THE U.S. CONSTITUTION
AND
RELATED DOCUMENTS

THE U.S. CONSTITUTION AND RELATED DOCUMENTS

★ ★ ★

Edited by
Stephen Brennan

Skyhorse Publishing

Skyhorse Publishing books may be purchased in bulk at special discounts for sales promotion, corporate gifts, fund-raising, or educational purposes. Special editions can also be created to specifications. For details, contact the Special Sales Department, Skyhorse Publishing, 307 West 36th Street, 11th Floor, New York, NY 10018 or info@skyhorsepublishing.com.

Skyhorse® and Skyhorse Publishing® are registered trademarks of Skyhorse Publishing, Inc.®, a Delaware corporation.

www.skyhorsepublishing.com

10 9 8 7 6 5 4 3 2 1

Library of Congress Cataloging-in-Publication Data is available on file.
ISBN: 978-1-61608-346-5

Printed in China

CONTENTS

★ ★ ★

INTRODUCTION

★ ★ ★

Nowadays when we look into the rear-view mirror of American history, we're often a little quick to attribute a kind of religious significance to the founding of our Republic. Some of this is the result of the words we habitually use to describe it. We call the Founders *Fathers,* as though they were Biblical patriarchs. We positively revere Washington, Jefferson, Madison, the Adams cousins, Ben Franklin, Patrick Henry, Tom Paine and the others, and in our collective imagination, we accord them something very like the status of saints. We regard the founding documents themselves as a sort of holy-writ, divinely inspired, like the writings of the old-time prophets. Over the last half-century in particular, we've taken to calling our written Constitution the "Miracle at Philadelphia," as though it was the hand of God, and not men's hands that did all that scribbling, as though our covenant was one with the Almighty, rather than one between ourselves.

With the language of faith so widely deployed, so prevalent in our civic discourse, it is no wonder we've mantled the whole business in a halo of light.

It might help for us to take a break from this better-than-two-hundred year-old hagiographic exercise, at least long enough to recognize the framers of our Constitution as a set of clear headed, hard bargaining, mostly plain spoken, pragmatic individuals. When these delegates to the Philadelphia Convention finally assembled in the late spring of 1787, they had little notion that they were doing God's work. The thought would not have occurred to them. Instead they had a number of very difficult jobs to do. And these difficulties were much more a matter of civics than of faith. Independence had been achieved, the Revolutionary War had been won, but the peace looked about to be lost. The country was coming apart, each state going its own way. Most of the delegates already recognized the crying need for efficacious, practical action; otherwise the young nation stood to lose all it had so far gained. Each of them had come to Philadelphia with strongly held positions and points of view. The Convention as a whole represented a vast divergence of imperatives, interests and traditions. But nearly all the delegates

Vintage engraved seal of the United States, 1886–1891

agreed—in fact most Americans agreed—that some kind of stronger union was desirable, if not absolutely necessary. This realization did not come all of a sudden, instead, it was a lesson already well learned by that first Greatest Generation. It had been true in the time of the Stamp and other Intolerable Acts. Unified action, by the people and among the colonies, had been the answer then, and each of the key documents since—the Articles of Association, *Common Sense,* the Declaration of Independence, and the Articles of Confederation—had all been further steps along this road. The Preamble to the Constitution made it explicit. "In order to form a more perfect Union…"

The United States Constitution—as it has come down to us today, amendments included—takes inspiration from, is a culmination of, and an answer to, all these earlier documents. I hope this look back at our most … all right, *sacred* documents, will permit the ordinary American a real sense of the generation-long struggle to found this nation, and an appreciation of just how well we've managed to keep faith with those original ideals. Objects in the rear-view mirror are nearer than they appear to be.

—Stephen Brennan

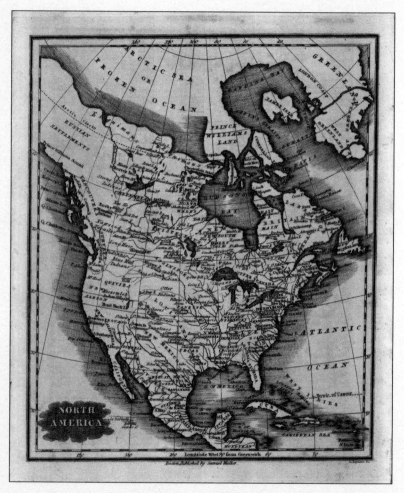

1799 Antique map of North America

THE ARTICLES OF ASSOCIATION

★ ★ ★

Perhaps the least appreciated document of the whole revolutionary struggle, the Articles of Association were the first real step towards union. In English law, Articles of Association served as a form of contract by which individuals agreed to act in concert towards a particular end or venture. Conceived in response to the British occupation and closing of the port of Boston, as well as to the other Intolerable Acts, this document allowed individuals to—as it were—sign up for the Revolution. It enumerated specific actions all signers were to undertake, and it road-mapped the rules and means by which this "contract" was to be enforced.

A page from the Articles of Association

THE ARTICLES OF ASSOCIATION

We, his Majesty's most loyal subjects, the delegates of the several colonies of New Hampshire, Massachusetts Bay, Rhode Island, Connecticut, New York, New Jersey, Pennsylvania, the three lower counties of New Castle, Kent and Sussex, on Delaware, Maryland, Virginia, North Carolina, and South Carolina, deputed to represent them in a continental Congress, held in the city of Philadelphia, on the 5th day of September, 1774, avowing our allegiance to his Majesty, our affection and regard for our fellow subjects in Great Britain and elsewhere, affected with the deepest anxiety, and most alarming apprehensions, at those grievances and distresses, with which his Majesty's American subjects are oppressed; and having taken under our most serious deliberation, the state of the whole continent, find, that the present unhappy situation of our affairs is occasioned by a ruinous system of colony administration, adopted by the British ministry about the year 1763, evidently calculated for enslaving these colonies, and, with them, the British empire.

In prosecution of which system, various acts of parliament have been passed, for raising a revenue in America, for depriving the American subjects, in many instances, of the constitutional trial by jury, exposing their lives to danger, by directing a new and illegal trial beyond the seas, for crimes alleged to have been committed in America: and in prosecution of the same system, several late, cruel, and oppressive acts have been passed, respecting the town of Boston and the Massachusetts Bay, and also an act for extending the province of Quebec, so as to border on the western frontiers of these colonies, establishing an arbitrary government therein, and discouraging the settlement of British subjects in that wide extended country; thus, by the influence of civil principles and ancient prejudices, to dispose the inhabitants to act with hostility against the free Protestant colonies, whenever a wicked ministry shall choose so to direct them.

To obtain redress of these grievances, which threaten destruction to the lives, liberty, and property of his majesty's subjects, in

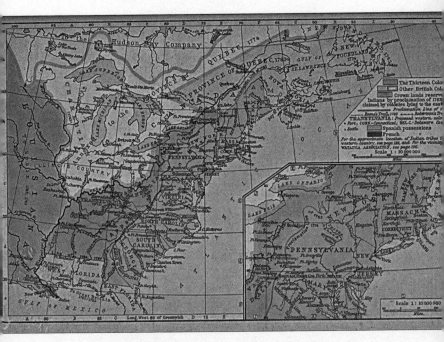

Map of the British Colonies from 1763 to 1776

Patrick Henry speaks to the Virginia House of Burgesses

North America, we are of opinion, that a non-importation, non-consumption, and non-exportation agreement, faithfully adhered to, will prove the most speedy, effectual, and peaceable measure: and, therefore, we do, for ourselves, and the inhabitants of the several colonies, whom we represent, firmly agree and associate, under the sacred ties of virtue, honor and love of our country, as follows:

1.   That from and after the first day of December next, we will not import, into British America, from Great Britain or

Ireland, any goods, wares, or merchandise whatsoever, or from any other place, any such goods, wares, or merchandise, as shall have been exported from Great Britain or Ireland; nor will we, after that day, import any East India tea from any part of the world; nor any molasses, syrups, paneles, coffee, or pimento, from the British plantations or from Dominica; nor wines from Madeira, or the Western Islands; nor foreign indigo.

    2.   We will neither import nor purchase, any slave imported after the first day of December next; after which time, we will wholly discontinue the slave trade, and will neither be concerned

Disputes aired at a colonial meeting

in it ourselves, nor will we hire our vessels, nor sell our commodities or manufactures to those who are concerned in it.

3. As a non-consumption agreement, strictly adhered to, will be an effectual security for the observation of the non-importation, we, as above, solemnly agree and associate, that, from this day, we will not purchase or use any tea, imported on account of the East India company, or any on which a duty has been or shall be paid; and from and after the first day of March next, we will not purchase or use any East India tea whatever; nor will we, nor shall any person for or under us, purchase or use any of those goods, wares, or merchandise, we have agreed not to import, which we shall know, or have cause to suspect, were imported after the first day of December, except such as come under the rules and directions of the tenth article hereafter mentioned.

4. The earnest desire we have, not to injure our fellow subjects in Great Britain, Ireland, or the West Indies, induces us to suspend a non-exportation, until the tenth day of September, 1775; at which time, if the said acts and parts of acts of the British parliament herein after mentioned are not repealed, we will not, directly or indirectly, export any merchandise or commodity whatsoever to Great Britain, Ireland, or the West Indies, except rice to Europe.

5. Such as are merchants, and use the British and Irish trade, will give orders, as soon as possible, to their factors, agents and correspondents, in Great Britain and Ireland, not to ship any goods to them, on any pretense whatsoever, as they cannot be

received in America; and if any merchant, residing in Great Britain or Ireland, shall directly or indirectly ship any goods, wares or merchandise, for America, in order to break the said non-importation agreement, or in any manner contravene the same, on such unworthy conduct being well attested, it ought to be made public; and, on the same being so done, we will not, from thenceforth, have any commercial connection with such merchant.

Shipping yard in Salem Massachusetts, 1770s

The Boston Tea Party

6. That such as are owners of vessels will give positive orders to their captains, or masters, not to receive on board their vessels any goods prohibited by the said non-importation agreement, on pain of immediate dismissal from their service.

7. We will use our utmost endeavors to improve the breed of sheep, and increase their number to the greatest extent; and to that end, we will kill them as seldom as may be, especially those of the most profitable kind; nor will we export any to the West Indies or elsewhere; and those of us, who are or may become overstocked with, or can conveniently spare any sheep, will dispose of them to our neighbors, especially to the poorer sort, on moderate terms.

8. We will, in our several stations, encourage frugality, economy, and industry, and promote agriculture, arts and the manufactures of this country, especially that of wool; and will discountenance and discourage every species of extravagance and dissipation, especially all horse racing, and all kinds of gaming, cock fighting, exhibitions of shows, plays, and other expensive diversions and entertainments; and on the death of any relation or

friend, none of us, or any of our families, will go into any further mourning-dress, than a black crape or ribbon on the arm or hat, for gentlemen, and a black ribbon and necklace for ladies, and we will discontinue the giving of gloves and scarves at funerals.

9.   Such as are vendors of goods or merchandise will not take advantage of the scarcity of goods, that may be occasioned by

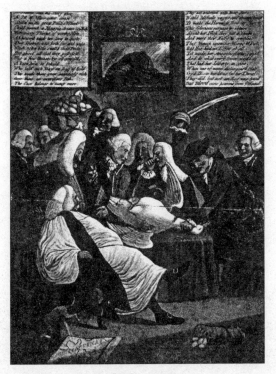

The Goose that Lays the Golden Eggs—British satire, 1770s. The King's Ministers Kill American Colonies.

this association, but will sell the same at the rates we have been respectively accustomed to do, for twelve months last past. And if any vendor of goods or merchandise shall sell any such goods on higher terms, or shall, in any manner, or by any device whatsoever violate or depart from this agreement, no person ought, nor will any of us deal with any such person, or his or her factor or agent, at any time thereafter, for any commodity whatever.

Thomas Rowlandson's depiction of a gambling den, 1792

10. In case any merchant, trader, or other person, shall import any goods or merchandise, after the first day of December, and before the first day of February next, the same ought forthwith, at the election of the owner, to be either re-shipped or delivered up to the committee of the county or town, wherein they shall be imported, to be stored at the risk of the importer, until the non-importation agreement shall cease, or be sold under the direction of the committee aforesaid; and in the last-mentioned case, the owner or owners of such goods shall be reimbursed out of the sales, the first cost and charges, the profit, if any, to be applied towards relieving and employing such poor inhabitants of the town of Boston, as are immediate sufferers by the Boston port-bill; and a particular account of all goods so returned, stored, or sold, to be inserted in the public papers; and if any goods or merchandises shall be imported after the said first day of February, the same ought forthwith to be sent back again, without breaking any of the packages thereof.

11. That a committee be chosen in every county, city, and town, by those who are qualified to vote for representatives in the legislature, whose business it shall be attentively to observe the conduct of all persons touching this association; and when it shall be made to appear, to the satisfaction of a majority of any such committee, that any person within the limits of their appointment has violated this association, that such majority do forthwith cause the truth of the case to be published in the gazette; to the end, that all such foes to the rights of British America may be publicly known, and universally condemned as the enemies of American liberty; and thenceforth we respectively will break off all dealings with him or her.

12. That the committee of correspondence, in the respective colonies, do frequently inspect the entries of their custom houses, and inform each other, from time to time, of the true state thereof, and of every other material circumstance that may occur relative to this association.

13. That all manufactures of this country be sold at reasonable prices, so that no undue advantage be taken of a future scarcity of goods.

Paul Revere's version of the Boston Massacre

14. And we do further agree and resolve, that we will have no trade, commerce, dealings or intercourse whatsoever, with any colony or province, in North America, which shall not accede to, or which shall hereafter violate this association, but will hold them as unworthy of the rights of freemen, and as inimical to the liberties of their country.

And we do solemnly bind ourselves and our constituents, under the ties aforesaid, to adhere to this association, until such parts of the several acts of parliament passed since the close of the last war, as impose or continue duties on tea, wine, molasses, syrups, paneles, coffee, sugar, pimento, indigo, foreign paper, glass, and painters' colors, imported into America, and extend the powers of the admiralty courts beyond their ancient limits, deprive the American subject of trial by jury, authorize the judge's certificate to indemnify the prosecutor from damages, that he might otherwise be liable to from a trial by his peers, require oppressive security from a claimant of ships or goods seized, before he shall be allowed to defend his property, are repealed. And until that part of the act of the 12 Geo. 3. chapter 24, entitled "An act for the better securing his majesty's dock-yards, magazines, ships, ammunition, and stores," by which any persons charged with committing any of the offenses therein described, in America, may be tried in any shire or county within the realm, is repealed and until the four acts, passed the last session of parliament, viz. that for stopping the port and blocking up the harbor of Boston—that for altering the charter and government of the Massachusetts Bay—and that which is entitled "An act for the better administration of justice, etc."—and that "for extending the limits of Quebec, etc." are repealed. And we recommend it to the provincial conventions, and to the committees in the

Battle at Bunker Hill

respective colonies, to establish such farther regulations as they may think proper, for carrying into execution this association.

The foregoing association being determined upon by the Congress, was ordered to be subscribed by the several members thereof; and thereupon, we have hereunto set our respective names accordingly.

In Congress, Philadelphia, October 20, 1774.

Signed, Peyton Randolph, President.

New Hampshire: Jno. Sullivan, Nathel. Folsom

Massachusetts Bay: Thomas Cushing, Saml. Adams, John Adams, Robt. Treat Paine

Rhode Island: Step. Hopkins, Sam. Ward

Connecticut: Elipht Dyer, Roger Sherman, Silas Deane

New York: Isaac Low, John Alsop, John Jay, Jas. Duane, Phil. Livingston, Wm. Floyd, Henry Wisner, S. Boerum

New Jersey: J. Kinsey, Wil. Livingston, Stepn. Crane, Richd. Smith, John De Hart

Pennsylvania: Jos. Galloway, John Dickinson, Cha. Humphreys, Thomas Mifflin, E. Biddle, John Morton, Geo. Ross

The Lower Counties New Castle: Geo: Ross, Caesar Rodney, Geo: Ross, Tho. M. Kean, Geo. Ross, Geo. Read

Maryland: Mat Tilghman, Ths. Johnson Junr., Wm. Paca, Samuel Chase

Virginia: Richard Henry Lee, Go. Washington, P. Henry Jr., Richard Bland, Benja. Harrison, Edmd. Pendleton

North Carolina: Will Hooper, Joseph Hewes, Rd. Caswell

South Carolina: Henry Middleton, Tho Lynch Christ, Gadsden J Rutledge, Edward Rutledge

COMMON SENSE

★ ★ ★

The pamphlet Common Sense was first published, anonymously, in early 1776. By year's end it had been re-printed numerous times, on presses all over the colonies, and was without a doubt the most popular publication—excepting perhaps the Bible—in all the Americas. Ever the idealist, Paine had signed over his copyright to the Continental Congress, and despite the work's immense popularity and its many editions, he never received a cent in royalties. But that was fine with Thomas Paine; he was a believer. He had revolution in his blood and he believed in human rights the way a preacher believes in Sunday. The simile is an apt one. Revolution and freedom were his religion and his church.

Written in plain, direct English prose, this work more than any other expressed the sense, now common among the majority of the colonists, that the time had come to break with the Mother Country.

We have here retained the original spelling, capitalization, and punctuation.

COMMON SENSE
BY THOMAS PAINE
INTRODUCTION TO THE THIRD EDITION

Perhaps the sentiments contained in the following pages, are not YET sufficiently fashionable to procure them general favour; a long habit of not thinking a thing WRONG, gives it a superficial appearance of being RIGHT, and raises at first a formidable outcry in defense of custom. But the tumult soon subsides. Time makes more converts than reason. As a long and violent abuse of power, is generally the Means of calling the right of it in question (and in Matters too which might never have been thought of, had not the Sufferers been aggravated into the inquiry) and as the King of

England hath undertaken in his OWN RIGHT, to support the Parliament in what he calls THEIRS, and as the good people of this country are grievously oppressed by the combination, they have an undoubted privilege to inquire into the pretensions of both, and equally to reject the usurpation of either. In

Painting of Thomas Paine by Auguste Millière, 1880

the following sheets, the author hath studiously avoided every thing which is personal among ourselves. Compliments as well as censure to individuals make no part thereof. The wise, and the worthy, need not the triumph of a pamphlet; and those whose sentiments are injudicious, or unfriendly, will cease of themselves unless too much pains are bestowed upon their conversion. The cause of America is in a great measure the cause of all mankind. Many circumstances hath, and will arise, which are not local, but universal, and through which the principles of all Lovers of Mankind are affected, and in the Event of which, their Affections are interested. The laying a Country desolate with Fire and Sword, declaring War against the natural rights of all Mankind, and extirpating the Defenders thereof from the Face of the Earth, is the Concern of every Man to whom Nature hath given the Power of feeling; of which Class, regardless of Party Censure, is the AUTHOR.

P. S. The Publication of this new Edition hath been delayed, with a View of taking notice (had it been necessary) of any Attempt to refute the Doctrine of Independence: As no Answer hath yet appeared, it is now presumed that none will, the Time needful for getting such a Performance ready for the Public being considerably past. Who the Author of this Production is, is wholly unnecessary to the Public, as the Object for Attention is the DOCTRINE ITSELF, not the MAN. Yet it may not be unnecessary to say, That he is unconnected with any

Colonial printing operation

Party, and under no sort of Influence public or private, but the influence of reason and principle.

Philadelphia, February 14, 1776

Of The Origin and Design of Government in General, With Concise Remarks on the English Constitution

SOME writers have so confounded society with government, as to leave little or no distinction between them; whereas they are not only different, but have different origins. Society is produced by our wants, and government by our wickedness; the former promotes our happiness POSITIVELY by uniting our affections, the latter NEGATIVELY by restraining our vices. The one encourages intercourse, the other creates distinctions. The first is a patron, the last a punisher.

Society in every state is a blessing, but Government, even in its best state, is but a necessary evil; in its worst state an intolerable one: for when we suffer, or are exposed to the same miseries BY A

GOVERNMENT, which we might expect in a country WITHOUT GOVERNMENT, our calamity is heightened by reflecting that we furnish the means by which we suffer. Government, like dress, is the badge of lost innocence; the palaces of kings are built upon the ruins of the bowers of paradise. For were the impulses of conscience clear, uniform and irresistibly obeyed, man would need no other lawgiver; but that not being the case, he finds it necessary to surrender up a part of his property to furnish means for the protection of the rest; and this he is induced to do by the same prudence which in every other case advises him, out of two evils to choose the least. Wherefore, security being the true design and end of government, it unanswerably follows that whatever form thereof appears most likely to ensure it to us, with the least expense and greatest benefit, is preferable to all others.

In order to gain a clear and just idea of the design and end of government, let us suppose a small number of persons settled in some sequestered part of the earth, unconnected with the rest; they will then represent the first peopling of any country, or of the world. In this state of natural liberty, society will be their first thought. A thousand motives will excite them thereto; the strength of one man is so unequal to his wants, and his mind so unfitted for perpetual solitude, that he is soon obliged to seek assistance and relief of another, who in his turn requires the same. Four or five united would be able to raise a tolerable dwelling in the midst of a wilderness, but one man might labour out the common period of life without accomplishing any thing; when he had felled his timber he could not remove it, nor erect it after it was removed; hunger in the mean time would urge him to quit his work, and every different want would call him a different way. Disease, nay even misfortune, would be death; for, though neither might be mortal, yet either would disable him from living, and reduce him to a state in which he might rather be said to perish than to die.

Thus necessity, like a gravitating power, would soon form our newly arrived emigrants into society, the reciprocal blessings of which would supersede, and render the obligations of law and government unnecessary while they remained perfectly just to each other; but as nothing but Heaven is impregnable to vice, it will unavoidably happen that in proportion as they surmount the first difficulties of emigration, which bound them together in a common cause, they will begin to relax in their duty and attachment to each other: and this remissness will point out the necessity of establishing some form of government to supply the defect of moral virtue.

Some convenient tree will afford them a State House, under the branches of which the whole Colony may assemble to deliberate on public matters. It is more than probable that their first laws will have the title only of Regulations and be enforced by no other penalty than public disesteem. In this first parliament every man by natural right will have a seat.

But as the Colony encreases, the public concerns will encrease likewise, and the distance at which the members may be separated, will render it too inconvenient for all of them to meet on every occasion as at first, when their number was small, their habitations near, and the public concerns few and trifling. This will point out the convenience of their consenting to leave the legislative part to be managed by a select number chosen from the whole body, who are supposed to have the same concerns at stake which those have who appointed them, and who will act in the same manner as the whole body would act were they present. If the colony continue encreasing, it will become necessary to augment the number of representatives, and that the interest of every part of the colony may be attended to, it will be found best to divide the whole into convenient parts, each part sending its proper number: and that the ELECTED might never form to themselves an interest separate from the ELECTORS, prudence will point out the propriety of having elections often: because as the ELECTED might by that means return and mix again with the general body of the ELECTORS in a few months, their fidelity to the public will be secured by the prudent reflection of not making a rod for themselves. And as this frequent interchange will establish a common interest with every part of the community, they will mutually and naturally support each other, and on this, (not on the unmeaning name of king,) depends the STRENGTH OF GOVERNMENT, AND THE HAPPINESS OF THE GOVERNED.

Here then is the origin and rise of government; namely, a mode rendered necessary by the inability of moral virtue to govern the world; here too is the design and end of government, viz. Freedom and security. And however our eyes may be dazzled with show, or our ears deceived by sound; however prejudice may warp our wills, or interest darken our understanding, the simple voice of nature and reason will say, 'tis right.

I draw my idea of the form of government from a principle in nature which no art can overturn, viz. that the more simple any thing is, the less liable it is to be disordered, and the easier repaired when disordered; and with this maxim in view I offer a few remarks on the so much boasted constitution of England. That it was noble for the dark and slavish times in which it was erected, is granted. When the world was overrun with tyranny the least remove therefrom was a glorious rescue. But that it is imperfect,

"Bostonians in Distress"—British Satire, 1770s

subject to convulsions, and incapable of producing what it seems to promise is easily demonstrated.

Absolute governments, (tho' the disgrace of human nature) have this advantage with them, they are simple; if the people suffer, they know the head from which their suffering springs; know likewise the remedy; and are not bewildered by a variety of causes and cures. But the constitution of England is so exceedingly complex, that the nation may suffer for years together without being able to discover in which part the fault lies; some will say in one and some in another, and every political physician will advise a different medicine.

I know it is difficult to get over local or long standing prejudices, yet if we will suffer ourselves to examine the component parts of the English Constitution, we shall find them to be the base remains of two ancient tyrannies, compounded with some new Republican materials.

First.—The remains of Monarchical tyranny in the person of the King.

Secondly.—The remains of Aristocratical tyranny in the persons of the Peers.

Thirdly.—The new Republican materials, in the persons of the Commons, on whose virtue depends the freedom of England.

The two first, by being hereditary, are independent of the People; wherefore in a CONSTITUTIONAL SENSE they contribute nothing towards the freedom of the State.

To say that the constitution of England is an UNION of three powers, reciprocally CHECKING each other, is farcical; either the words have no meaning, or they are flat contradictions.

To say that the Commons is a check on the King, pressupposes two things.

First.—That the King it not to be trusted without being looked after; or in other words, that a thirst for absolute power is the natural disease of monarchy.

Secondly.—That the Commons, by being appointed for that purpose, are either wiser or more worthy of confidence than the Crown.

But as the same constitution which gives the Commons a power to check the King by withholding the supplies, gives afterwards the King a power to check the Commons, by empowering him to reject their other bills; it again supposes that the King is wiser than those whom it has already supposed to be wiser than him. A mere absurdity!

There is something exceedingly ridiculous in the composition of Monarchy; it first excludes a man from the means of information, yet empowers him to act in cases where the highest judg-

Military portrait of King George IV, King George III, and Frederick, Duke of York and Albany, by Charles Tomkins

ment is required. The state of a king shuts him from the World, yet the business of a king requires him to know it thoroughly; wherefore the different parts, by unnaturally opposing and destroying each other, prove the whole character to be absurd and useless.

Some writers have explained the English constitution thus: the King, say they, is one, the people another; the Peers are a house in behalf of the King, the commons in behalf of the people; but this hath all the distinctions of a house divided against itself; and though the expressions be pleasantly arranged, yet when examined they appear idle and ambiguous; and it will always happen, that the nicest construction that words are capable of, when applied to the description of something which either cannot exist, or is too incomprehensible to be within the compass of description, will be words of sound only, and though they may amuse the ear, they cannot inform the mind: for this explanation includes a previous question, viz. HOW CAME THE KING BY A POWER WHICH THE PEOPLE ARE AFRAID TO TRUST, AND ALWAYS OBLIGED TO CHECK? Such a power could not be the gift of a wise people, neither can any power, WHICH NEEDS CHECKING, be from God; yet the provision which the constitution makes supposes such a power to exist.

But the provision is unequal to the task; the means either cannot or will not accomplish the end, and the whole affair is a Felo de se: for as the greater weight will always carry up the less, and as all the wheels of a machine are put in motion by one, it only remains to know which power in the constitution has the most weight, for that will govern: and tho' the others, or a part of them, may clog, or, as the phrase is, check the rapidity of its motion, yet so long as they cannot stop it, their endeavours will be ineffectual:

The first moving power will at last have its way, and what it wants in speed is supplied by time.

That the crown is this overbearing part in the English constitution needs not be mentioned, and that it derives its whole consequence merely from being the giver of places and pensions is self-evident; wherefore, though we have been wise enough to shut and lock a door against absolute Monarchy, we at the same time have been foolish enough to put the Crown in possession of the key.

The prejudice of Englishmen, in favour of their own government, by King, Lords and Commons, arises as much or more from national pride than reason. Individuals are undoubtedly safer in England than in some other countries: but the will of the king is as much the law of the land in Britain as in France, with this difference, that instead of proceeding directly from his mouth, it is handed to the people under the formidable shape of an act of parliament. For the fate of Charles the First hath only made kings more subtle—not more just.

Wherefore, laying aside all national pride and prejudice in favour of modes and forms, the plain truth is that IT IS WHOLLY OWING TO THE CONSTITUTION OF THE PEOPLE, AND NOT TO THE CONSTITUTION OF THE GOVERNMENT that the crown is not as oppressive in England as in Turkey.

An inquiry into the CONSTITUTIONAL ERRORS in the English form of government, is at this time highly necessary; for as we are never in a proper condition of doing justice to others, while we continue under the influence of some leading partiality, so neither are we capable of doing it to ourselves while we remain fettered by any obstinate prejudice. And as a man who is attached to a prostitute is unfitted to choose or judge of a wife, so any prepossession in favour of a rotten constitution of government will disable us from discerning a good one.

Of Monarchy and Hereditary Succession

MANKIND being originally equals in the order of creation, the equality could only be destroyed by some subsequent circumstance: the distinctions of rich and poor may in a great measure be accounted for, and that without having recourse to the harsh ill-sounding names of oppression and avarice. Oppression is often the CONSEQUENCE, but seldom or never the MEANS of riches; and tho' avarice will preserve a man from being necessitously poor, it generally makes him too timorous to be wealthy.

But there is another and great distinction for which no truly natural or religious reason can be assigned, and that is the distinction of men into KINGS and SUBJECTS. Male and female are the distinctions of nature, good and bad the distinctions of Heaven; but how a race of men came into the world so exalted above the rest, and distinguished like some new species, is worth inquiring into, and whether they are the means of happiness or of misery to mankind.

In the early ages of the world, according to the scripture chronology there were no kings; the consequence of which was, there were no wars; it is the pride of kings which throws mankind into confusion. Holland, without a king hath enjoyed more peace for this last century than any of the monarchical governments in Europe. Antiquity favours the same remark; for the quiet and rural lives of the first Patriarchs have a snappy something in them, which vanishes when we come to the history of Jewish royalty.

Government by kings was first introduced into the world by the Heathens, from whom the children of Israel copied the custom. It was the most prosperous invention the Devil ever set on foot for the promotion of idolatry. The Heathens paid divine honours to their deceased kings, and the Christian World hath improved on the plan by doing the same to their living ones. How impious is the

Thomas Paine surrounded by injustices and standing on lables, representing morals and justices, defending measures taken in revolutionary France and appealing to the English to overthrow their monarchy and reorganize a republic, 1792

title of sacred Majesty applied to a worm, who in the midst of his splendor is crumbling into dust!

As the exalting one man so greatly above the rest cannot be justified on the equal rights of nature, so neither can it be defended on the authority of scripture; for the will of the Almighty as declared by Gideon, and the prophet Samuel, expressly disapproves of government by Kings.

All anti-monarchical parts of scripture have been very smoothly glossed over in monarchical governments, but they undoubtedly merit the attention of countries which have their governments yet to form. "Render unto Cesar the things which are Cesar's" is the scripture doctrine of courts, yet it is no support of monarchical government, for the Jews at that time were without a king, and in a state of vassalage to the Romans.

Near three thousand years passed away, from the Mosaic account of the creation, till the Jews under a national delusion requested a king. Till then their form of government (except in extraordinary cases where the Almighty interposed) was a kind of Republic, administered by a judge and the elders of the tribes. Kings they had none, and it was held sinful to acknowledge any being under that title but the Lord of Hosts. And when a man seriously reflects on the idolatrous homage which is paid to the persons of kings, he need not wonder that the Almighty, ever jealous of his honour, should disapprove a form of government which so impiously invades the prerogative of Heaven.

Monarchy is ranked in scripture as one of the sins of the Jews, for which a curse in reserve is denounced against them. The history of that transaction is worth attending to.

The children of Israel being oppressed by the Midianites, Gideon marched against them with a small army, and victory thro' the divine interposition decided in his favour. The Jews, elate with success, and attributing it to the generalship of Gideon, proposed making him a king, saying, "Rule thou over us, thou and thy son, and thy son's son." Here was temptation in its fullest extent; not a kingdom only, but an hereditary one; but Gideon in the piety of his soul replied, "I will not rule over you, neither shall my son rule over you. THE LORD SHALL RULE OVER YOU." Words need not be more explicit: Gideon doth not decline the honour, but denieth their right to give it; neither doth he compliment them with invented declarations of his thanks, but in the positive style of a prophet charges them with disaffection to their proper Sovereign, the King of Heaven.

About one hundred and thirty years after this, they fell again into the same error. The hankering which the Jews had for the idolatrous customs of the Heathens, is something exceedingly unaccountable; but so it was, that laying hold of the misconduct of Samuel's two sons, who were intrusted with some secular concerns, they came in an abrupt and clamorous manner to Samuel, saying, "Behold thou art old, and thy sons walk not in thy ways, now make us a king to judge us like all the other nations." And here we cannot observe but that their motives were bad, viz. that they might be LIKE unto other nations, i.e. the Heathens, whereas their true glory lay in being as much UNLIKE them as possible. "But the thing displeased Samuel when they said, give us a King to judge us; and Samuel prayed unto the Lord, and the Lord said unto Samuel, hearken unto the voice of the people in all that they say unto thee, for they have not rejected thee, but they have rejected me, THAT I SHOULD NOT REIGN OVER THEM. According to all the works which they have done since the day that I brought them up out of Egypt even unto this day, wherewith they have forsaken me, and served other Gods: so do they also unto thee. Now therefore hearken unto their voice, howbeit, protest solemnly unto them and show them the manner of the King that shall reign over them," i.e. not of any particular King, but the general manner of the Kings of the earth whom Israel was so eagerly copying after. And notwithstanding the great distance of time and difference of manners, the character is still in fashion. "And Samuel told all the words of the Lord unto the people, that asked of him a King. And he said, This shall be the manner of the King that shall reign over you. He will take your sons and appoint them for himself for his chariots and to be his horsemen, and some shall run before his chariots" (this description agrees with the present mode of impressing men) "and he will appoint him captains over thousands and captains over fifties, will set them to clear his ground and to reap his harvest, and to make his instruments of war, and instruments of his chariots. And he will take your daughters to be confectionaries, and to be cooks, and to be bakers" (this describes the expense and luxury as well as the oppression of Kings) "and he will take your fields and your vineyards, and your olive yards, even the best of them, and give them to his servants. And he will take the tenth of your seed, and of your vineyards, and give them to his officers and to his servants" (by which we see that bribery, corruption, and favouritism, are the standing vices of Kings) "and he will take the tenth of your men servants, and your maid servants, and your goodliest young men, and your asses, and put them to his work: and he will take the tenth of your sheep, and ye shall be his servants, and ye shall cry out in that day because of your king which ye shall have chosen, AND THE LORD WILL NOT HEAR YOU IN THAT DAY." This accounts for the continuation of Monarchy; neither do the characters of the few good kings which have lived since, either sanctify the title, or blot out the sinfulness of the origin; the high encomium of David takes no notice of him OFFICIALLY AS A KING, but only as a MAN after God's own heart. "Nevertheless the people refused to obey the voice of Samuel, and they said, Nay, but we will have a king over us, that we may be like all the nations, and that our king may judge us, and go out before us and fight our battles." Samuel continued to reason with them but to no purpose; he set before them their ingratitude, but all would not avail; and seeing them fully bent on their folly, he cried out, "I will call unto the Lord, and he shall send thunder and rain" (which was then a punishment, being in the time of wheat harvest) "that ye may perceive and see that your wickedness is great which ye have done in the sight of the Lord, IN ASKING YOU A KING. So Samuel called unto the Lord, and the Lord sent thunder and rain that day, and all the people greatly feared the Lord and Samuel. And all the people said unto Samuel, Pray for thy servants unto the Lord thy God that we die not, for WE HAVE ADDED UNTO OUR SINS THIS EVIL, TO ASK A KING." These portions of scripture are direct and positive. They admit of no equivocal construction. That the Almighty hath here entered his protest against monarchical government is true, or the scripture is false. And a man hath good

An illustration of King George III from an issue of Harper's Monthly Magazine, *April 1883*

reason to believe that there is as much of kingcraft as priestcraft in withholding the scripture from the public in popish countries. For monarchy in every instance is the popery of government.

To the evil of monarchy we have added that of hereditary succession; and as the first is a degradation and lessening of ourselves, so the second, claimed as a matter of right, is an insult and imposition on posterity. For all men being originally equals, no one by birth could have a right to set up his own family in perpetual preference to all others for ever, and tho' himself might deserve some decent degree of honours of his contemporaries, yet his descendants might be far too unworthy to inherit them. One of the strongest natural proofs of the folly of hereditary right in Kings, is that nature disapproves it, otherwise she would not so frequently turn it into ridicule, by giving mankind an ASS FOR A LION.

Secondly, as no man at first could possess any other public honors than were bestowed upon him, so the givers of those honors could have no power to give away the right of posterity, and though they might say "We choose you for our head," they could not without manifest injustice to their children say "that your children and your children's children shall reign over ours forever." Because such an unwise, unjust, unnatural compact might (perhaps) in the next succession put them under the government of a rogue or a fool. Most wise men in their private sentiments have ever treated hereditary right with contempt; yet it is one of those evils which when once established is not easily removed: many submit from fear, others from superstition, and the more powerful part shares with the king the plunder of the rest.

This is supposing the present race of kings in the world to have had an honorable origin: whereas it is more than probable, that, could we take off the dark covering of antiquity and trace them to their first rise, we should find the first of them nothing better than the principal ruffian of some restless gang, whose savage manners of pre-eminence in subtilty obtained him the title of chief among plunderers; and who by increasing in power and extending his depredations, overawed the quiet and defenseless to purchase their safety by frequent contributions. Yet his electors could have no idea of giving hereditary right to his descendants, because such a perpetual exclusion of themselves was incompatible with the free and restrained principles they professed to live by. Wherefore, hereditary succession in the early ages of monarchy could not take place as a matter of claim, but as something casual or complemental; but as few or no records were extant in those days, the traditionary history stuff'd with fables, it was very easy, after the lapse of a few generations, to trump up some superstitious tale conveniently timed, Mahomet-like, to cram hereditary right down the throats of the vulgar. Perhaps the disorders which threatened, or seemed to threaten, on the decease of a leader and the choice of a new one (for elections among ruffians could not be very orderly) induced many at first to favour hereditary pretensions; by which means it happened, as it hath happened since, that what at first was submitted to as a convenience was afterwards claimed as a right.

England since the conquest hath known some few good monarchs, but groaned beneath a much larger number of bad ones: yet no man in his senses can say that their claim under William the Conqueror is a very honourable one. A French bastard landing with an armed Banditti and establishing himself king of England against the consent of the natives, is in plain terms a very paltry rascally original. It certainly hath no divinity in it. However it is needless to spend much time in exposing the folly of hereditary right; if there are any so weak as to believe it, let them promiscuously worship the Ass and the Lion, and welcome. I shall neither copy their humility, nor disturb their devotion.

Yet I should be glad to ask how they suppose kings came at first? The question admits but of three answers, viz. either by lot, by election, or by usurpation. If the first king was taken by lot, it establishes a precedent for the next, which excludes hereditary succession. Saul was by lot, yet the succession was not hereditary, neither does it appear from that transaction that there was any intention it ever should. If the first king of any country was by election, that likewise establishes a precedent for the next; for to say, that the right of all future generations is taken away, by the act of the first electors, in their choice not only of a king but of a family of kings for ever, hath no parallel in or out of scripture but the doctrine of original sin, which supposes the free will of all men lost in Adam; and from such comparison, and it will admit of no other, hereditary succession can derive no glory. For as in Adam all sinned, and as in the first electors all men obeyed; as in the one all mankind were subjected to Satan, and in the other to sovereignty; as our innocence was lost in the first, and our authority in the last; and as both disable us from re-assuming some former state and privilege, it unanswerably follows that original sin and hereditary succession are parallels. Dishonourable rank! inglorious connection! yet the most subtle sophist cannot produce a juster simile.

As to usurpation, no man will be so hardy as to defend it; and that William the Conqueror was an usurper is a fact not to be contradicted. The plain truth is, that the antiquity of English monarchy will not bear looking into.

But it is not so much the absurdity as the evil of hereditary succession which concerns mankind. Did it ensure a race of good and wise men it would have the seal of divine authority, but as it opens a door to the FOOLISH, the WICKED, and the IMPROPER, it hath in it the nature of oppression. Men who look upon themselves born to reign, and others to obey, soon grow insolent. Selected from the rest of mankind, their minds are early poisoned by importance; and the world they act in differs so materially from the world at large, that they have but little opportunity of knowing its true interests, and when they succeed in the government are frequently the most ignorant and unfit of any throughout the dominions.

Another evil which attends hereditary succession is, that the throne is subject to be possessed by a minor at any age; all which time the regency acting under the cover of a king have every opportunity and inducement to betray their trust. The same national misfortune happens when a king worn out with age and infirmity enters the last stage of human weakness. In both these cases the public becomes a prey to every miscreant who can tamper successfully with the follies either of age or infancy.

The most plausible plea which hath ever been offered in favor of hereditary succession is, that it preserves a nation from civil wars; and were this true, it would be weighty; whereas it is the most bare-faced falsity ever imposed upon mankind. The whole history of England disowns the fact. Thirty kings and two minors have reigned in that distracted kingdom since the conquest, in which time there has been (including the revolution) no less than eight civil wars and nineteen Rebellions. Wherefore instead of making for peace, it makes against it, and destroys the very foundation it seems to stand upon.

The contest for monarchy and succession, between the houses of York and Lancaster, laid England in a scene of blood for many years. Twelve pitched battles besides skirmishes and sieges were fought between Henry and Edward. Twice was Henry prisoner to Edward, who in his turn was prisoner to Henry. And so uncertain is the fate of war and the temper of a nation, when nothing but personal matters are the ground of a quarrel, that Henry was taken in triumph from a prison to a palace, and Edward obliged to fly from a palace to a foreign land; yet, as sudden transitions of temper are seldom lasting, Henry in his turn was driven from the throne, and Edward re-called to succeed him. The parliament always following the strongest side.

This contest began in the reign of Henry the Sixth, and was not entirely extinguished till Henry the Seventh, in whom the families were united. Including a period of 67 years, viz. from 1422 to 1489.

In short, monarchy and succession have laid (not this or that kingdom only) but the world in blood and ashes. 'Tis a form of government which the word of God bears testimony against, and blood will attend it.

Windsor Castle today

If we enquire into the business of a King, we shall find that in some countries they may have none; and after sauntering away their lives without pleasure to themselves or advantage to the nation, withdraw from the scene, and leave their successors to tread the same idle round. In absolute monarchies the whole weight of business civil and military lies on the King; the children of Israel in their request for a king urged this plea, "that he may judge us, and go out before us and fight our battles." But in countries where he is neither a Judge nor a General, as in England, a man would be puzzled to know what IS his business.

The nearer any government approaches to a Republic, the less business there is for a King. It is somewhat difficult to find a proper name for the government of England. Sir William Meredith calls it a Republic; but in its present state it is unworthy of the name, because the corrupt influence of the Crown, by having all the places in its disposal, hath so effectually swallowed up the power, and eaten out the virtue of the House of Commons (the Republican part in the constitution) that the government of England is nearly as monarchical as that of France or Spain. Men fall out with names without understanding them. For 'tis the Republican and not the Monarchical part of the Constitution of England which Englishmen glory in, viz. the liberty of choosing an House of Commons from out of their own body—and it is easy to see that when Republican virtues fail, slavery ensues. Why is the constitution of England sickly, but because monarchy hath poisoned the Republic; the Crown hath engrossed the Commons.

In England a King hath little more to do than to make war and give away places; which, in plain terms, is to empoverish the nation and set it together by the ears. A pretty business indeed for a man to be allowed eight hundred thousand sterling a year for, and worshipped into the bargain! Of more worth is one honest man to society, and in the sight of God, than all the crowned ruffians that ever lived.

Thoughts on the Present State of American Affairs

IN the following pages I offer nothing more than simple facts, plain arguments, and common sense: and have no other preliminaries to settle with the reader, than that he will divest himself of prejudice and prepossession, and suffer his reason and his feelings to determine for themselves: that he will put on, or rather that he will not put off, the true character of a man, and generously enlarge his views beyond the present day.

Volumes have been written on the subject of the struggle between England and America. Men of all ranks have embarked in the controversy, from different motives, and with various designs; but all have been ineffectual, and the period of debate is closed. Arms as the last resource decide the contest; the appeal was the choice of the King, and the Continent has accepted the challenge.

It hath been reported of the late Mr. Pelham (who tho' an able minister was not without his faults) that on his being attacked in the House of Commons on the score that his measures were only of a temporary kind,

An illustration of Benjamin Franklin from an issue of Harper's Monthly Magazine, *April 1883*

replied, "THEY WILL LAST MY TIME." Should a thought so fatal and unmanly possess the Colonies in the present contest, the name of ancestors will be remembered by future generations with detestation.

The Sun never shined on a cause of greater worth. 'Tis not the affair of a City, a County, a Province, or a Kingdom; but of a Continent—of at least one-eighth part of the habitable Globe. 'Tis not the concern of a day, a year, or an age; posterity are virtually involved in the contest, and will be more or less affected even to the end of time, by the proceedings now. Now is the seed-time of Continental union, faith and honour. The least fracture now will be like a name engraved with the point of a pin on the tender rind of a young oak; the wound would enlarge with the tree, and posterity read it in full grown characters.

By referring the matter from argument to arms, a new era for politics is struck—a new method of thinking hath arisen. All plans, proposals, &c. prior to the nineteenth of April, i.e. to the commencement of hostilities, are like the almanacks of the last year; which tho' proper then, are superseded and useless now. Whatever was advanced by the advocates on either side of the question then, terminated in one and the same point, viz. a union with Great Britain; the only difference between the parties was the method of effecting it; the one proposing force, the other friendship; but it hath so far happened that the first hath failed, and the second hath withdrawn her influence.

As much hath been said of the advantages of reconciliation, which, like an agreeable dream, hath passed away and left us as we were, it is but right that we should examine the contrary side of the argument, and enquire into some of the many material injuries which these Colonies sustain, and always will sustain, by being connected with and dependent on Great Britain. To examine that connection and dependence, on the principles of nature and common sense, to see what we have to trust to, if separated, and what we are to expect, if dependent.

I have heard it asserted by some, that as America has flourished under her former connection with Great Britain, the same connection is necessary towards her future happiness, and will always have the same effect. Nothing can be more fallacious than this kind of argument. We may as well assert that because a child has thrived upon milk, that it is never to have meat, or that the first twenty years of our lives is to become a precedent for the next twenty. But even this is admitting more than is true; for I answer roundly that America would have flourished as much, and probably much more, had no European power taken any notice of her. The commerce by which she hath enriched herself are the necessaries of life, and will always have a market while eating is the custom of Europe.

But she has protected us, say some. That she hath engrossed us is true, and defended the Continent at our expense as well as her own, is admitted; and she would have defended Turkey from the same motive, viz.—for the sake of trade and dominion.

Alas! we have been long led away by ancient prejudices and made large sacrifices to superstition. We have boasted the protection of Great Britain, without considering, that her motive was INTEREST not ATTACHMENT; and that she did not protect us from OUR ENEMIES on OUR ACCOUNT; but from HER ENEMIES on HER OWN ACCOUNT, from those who had no quarrel with us on any OTHER ACCOUNT, and who will always be our enemies on the SAME ACCOUNT. Let Britain waive her pretensions to the Continent, or the Continent throw off the dependence, and we should be at peace with France and Spain, were they at war with Britain. The miseries of Hanover last war ought to warn us against connections.

It hath lately been asserted in parliament, that the Colonies have no relation to each other but through the Parent Country, i.e. that Pennsylvania and the Jerseys and so on for the rest, are sister Colonies by the way of England; this is certainly a very roundabout way of proving relationship, but it is the nearest and only true way of proving enmity (or enemyship, if I may so call it.) France and

Vintage map of the world hemispheres, created by Frederick Dewit, 1668

Spain never were, nor perhaps ever will be, our enemies as AMER-ICANS, but as our being the SUBJECTS OF GREAT BRITAIN.

But Britain is the parent country, say some. Then the more shame upon her conduct. Even brutes do not devour their young, nor savages make war upon their families. Wherefore, the assertion, if true, turns to her reproach; but it happens not to be true, or only partly so, and the phrase PARENT OR MOTHER COUNTRY hath been jesuitically adopted by the King and his parasites, with a low papistical design of gaining an unfair bias on the credulous weakness of our minds. Europe, and not England, is the parent country of America. This new World hath been the asylum for the persecuted lovers of civil and religious liberty from EVERY PART of Europe. Hither have they fled, not from the tender embraces of the mother, but from the cruelty of the monster; and it is so far true of England, that the same tyranny which drove the first emigrants from home, pursues their descendants still.

In this extensive quarter of the globe, we forget the narrow limits of three hundred and sixty miles (the extent of England) and carry our friendship on a larger scale; we claim brotherhood with every European Christian, and triumph in the generosity of the sentiment.

It is pleasant to observe by what regular gradations we surmount the force of local prejudices, as we enlarge our acquaintance with the World. A man born in any town in England divided into parishes, will naturally associate most with his fellow parishioners (because their interests in many cases will be common) and distinguish him by the name of NEIGHBOR; if he meet him but a few miles from home, he drops the narrow idea of a street, and salutes him by the name of TOWNSMAN; if he travel out of the county and meet him in any other, he forgets the minor divisions of street and town, and calls him COUNTRYMAN, i.e. COUNTYMAN; but if in their foreign excursions they should associate in France, or any other part of EUROPE, their local remembrance would be enlarged into that of ENGLISHMEN. And by a just parity of reasoning, all Europeans meeting in America, or any other quarter of the globe, are COUNTRYMEN; for England, Holland, Germany, or Sweden, when compared with the whole, stand in the same places on the larger scale, which the divisions of street, town, and county do on the smaller ones; Distinctions too limited for

Big Ben and the Houses of Parliament today

Continental minds. Not one third of the inhabitants, even of this province, [Pennsylvania], are of English descent. Wherefore, I reprobate the phrase of Parent or Mother Country applied to England only, as being false, selfish, narrow and ungenerous.

But, admitting that we were all of English descent, what does it amount to? Nothing. Britain, being now an open enemy, extinguishes every other name and title: and to say that reconciliation is our duty, is truly farcical. The first king of England, of the present line (William the Conqueror) was a Frenchman, and half the peers of England are descendants from the same country; wherefore, by the same method of reasoning, England ought to be governed by France.

Much hath been said of the united strength of Britain and the Colonies, that in conjunction they might bid defiance to the world. But this is mere presumption; the fate of war is uncertain, neither do the expressions mean anything; for this continent would never suffer itself to be drained of inhabitants, to support the British arms in either Asia, Africa, or Europe.

Besides, what have we to do with setting the world at defiance? Our plan is commerce, and that, well attended to, will secure us the peace and friendship of all Europe; because it is the interest of all Europe to have America a free port. Her trade will always be a protection, and her barrenness of gold and silver secure her from invaders.

I challenge the warmest advocate for reconciliation to show a single advantage that this continent can reap by being connected with Great Britain. I repeat the challenge; not a single advantage is derived. Our corn will fetch its price in any market in Europe, and our imported goods must be paid for buy them where we will.

But the injuries and disadvantages which we sustain by that connection, are without number; and our duty to mankind at large, as well as to ourselves, instruct us to renounce the alliance: because, any submission to, or dependence on, Great Britain, tends directly to involve this Continent in European wars and quarrels, and set us at variance with nations who would otherwise seek our friendship, and against whom we have neither anger nor complaint. As Europe is our market for trade, we ought to form no partial connection with any part of it. It is the true interest of America to steer clear of European contentions, which she never can do, while, by her dependence on Britain, she is made the makeweight in the scale of British politics.

Europe is too thickly planted with Kingdoms to be long at peace, and whenever a war breaks out between England and any foreign power, the trade of America goes to ruin, BECAUSE OF HER CONNECTION WITH BRITAIN. The next war may not turn out like the last, and should it not, the advocates for reconciliation now will be wishing for separation then, because neutrality in that case would be a safer convoy than a man of war. Every thing that is right or reasonable pleads for separation. The blood of the slain, the weeping voice of nature cries, 'TIS TIME TO PART. Even the distance at which the Almighty hath placed England and America is a strong and natural proof that the authority of the one over the other, was never the design of Heaven. The time likewise at which the Continent was discovered, adds weight to the argument, and the manner in which it was peopled, encreases the force of it. The Reformation was preceded by the discovery of America: As if the Almighty graciously meant to open a sanctuary to the persecuted in future years, when home should afford neither friendship nor safety.

The authority of Great Britain over this continent, is a form of government, which sooner or later must have an end: And a serious mind can draw no true pleasure by looking forward, under the painful and positive conviction that what he calls "the present constitution" is merely temporary. As parents, we can have no joy, knowing that this government is not sufficiently lasting to ensure any thing which we may bequeath to posterity: And by a plain method of argument, as we are running the next generation into debt, we ought to do the work of it, otherwise we use them meanly and pitifully. In order to discover the line of our duty rightly, we should take our children in our hand, and fix our station a few years farther into life; that eminence will present a prospect which a few present fears and prejudices conceal from our sight.

Early copy of Common Sense

Though I would carefully avoid giving unnecessary offence, yet I am inclined to believe, that all those who espouse the doctrine of reconciliation, may be included within the following descriptions. Interested men, who are not to be trusted, weak men who CANNOT see, prejudiced men who will not see, and a certain set of moderate men who think better of the European world than it deserves; and this last class, by an ill-judged deliberation, will be the cause of more calamities to this Continent than all the other three.

It is the good fortune of many to live distant from the scene of present sorrow; the evil is not sufficiently brought to their doors to make them feel the precariousness with which all American property is possessed. But let our imaginations transport us a few moments to Boston; that seat of wretchedness will teach us wisdom, and instruct us for ever to renounce a power in whom we can have no trust. The inhabitants of that unfortunate city who but a few months ago were in ease and affluence, have now no other alternative than to stay and starve, or turn out to beg. Endangered by the fire of their friends if they continue within the city and plundered by the soldiery if they leave it, in their present situation they are prisoners without the hope of redemption, and in a general attack for their relief they would be exposed to the fury of both armies.

Men of passive tempers look somewhat lightly over the offences of Great Britain, and, still hoping for the best, are apt to call out, "Come, come, we shall be friends again for all this." But examine the passions and feelings of mankind: bring the doctrine of reconciliation to the touchstone of nature, and then tell me whether you can hereafter love, honour, and faithfully serve the power that hath carried fire and sword into your land? If you cannot do all these, then are you only deceiving yourselves, and by your delay bringing ruin upon posterity. Your future connection with Britain, whom you can neither love nor honour, will be forced and unnatural, and being formed only on the plan of present convenience, will in a little time fall into a relapse more wretched than the first. But if you say, you can still pass the violations over, then I ask, hath your house been burnt? Hath your property been destroyed before your face? Are your wife and children destitute of a bed to lie on, or bread to live on? Have you lost a parent or a child by their hands, and yourself the ruined and wretched survivor? If you have not, then are you not a judge of those who have. But if you have, and can still shake hands with the murderers, then are you unworthy the name of husband, father, friend or lover, and whatever may be your rank or title in life, you have the heart of a coward, and the spirit of a sycophant.

British coat of arms carved out of limestone

This is not inflaming or exaggerating matters, but trying them by those feelings and affections which nature justifies, and without which we should be incapable of discharging the social duties of life, or enjoying the felicities of it. I mean not to exhibit horror for the purpose of provoking revenge, but to awaken us from fatal and unmanly slumbers, that we may pursue determinately some fixed object. It is not in the power of Britain or of Europe to conquer America, if she do not conquer herself by delay and timidity. The present winter is worth an age if rightly employed, but if lost or neglected, the whole continent will partake of the misfortune; and there is no punishment which that man will not deserve, be he who, or what, or where he will, that may be the means of sacrificing a season so precious and useful.

It is repugnant to reason, to the universal order of things, to all examples from former ages, to suppose that this continent can longer remain subject to any external power. The most sanguine in Britain does not think so. The utmost stretch of human wisdom cannot, at this time, compass a plan short of separation, which can promise the continent even a year's security. Reconciliation is now a fallacious dream. Nature hath deserted the connexion, and Art cannot supply her place. For, as Milton wisely expresses, "never can true reconcilement grow where wounds of deadly hate have pierced so deep."

Every quiet method for peace hath been ineffectual. Our prayers have been rejected with disdain; and only tended to convince us, that nothing flatters vanity, or confirms obstinacy in Kings more than repeated petitioning—and nothing hath contributed more than that very measure to make the Kings of Europe absolute: Witness Denmark and Sweden. Wherefore, since nothing but blows will do, for God's sake, let us come to a final separation, and not leave the next generation to be cutting throats, under the violated unmeaning names of parent and child.

To say, they will never attempt it again is idle and visionary, we thought so at the repeal of the stamp act, yet a year or two undeceived us; as well may we suppose that nations, which have been once defeated, will never renew the quarrel.

As to government matters, it is not in the power of Britain to do this continent justice: The business of it will soon be too weighty, and intricate, to be managed with any tolerable degree of convenience, by a power so distant from us, and so very ignorant of us; for if they cannot conquer us, they cannot govern us. To be always running three or four thousand miles with a tale or a petition, waiting four or five months for an answer, which when obtained requires five or six more to explain it in, will in a few years be looked upon as folly and childishness—there was a time when it was proper, and there is a proper time for it to cease.

Small islands not capable of protecting themselves, are the proper objects for kingdoms to take under their care; but there is something very absurd, in supposing a continent to be perpetually governed by an island. In no instance hath nature made the satellite larger than its primary planet, and as England and America, with respect to each other, reverses the common order of nature, it is evident they belong to different systems: England to Europe, America to itself.

I am not induced by motives of pride, party, or resentment to espouse the doctrine of separation and independence; I am clearly, positively, and conscientiously persuaded that it is the true interest of this continent to be so; that every thing short of that is mere patchwork, that it can afford no lasting felicity,—that it is leaving the sword to our children, and shrinking back at a time, when, a little more, a little farther, would have rendered this continent the glory of the earth.

As Britain hath not manifested the least inclination towards a compromise, we may be assured that no terms can be obtained worthy the acceptance of the continent, or any ways equal to the expense of blood and treasure we have been already put to.

The object, contended for, ought always to bear some just proportion to the expense. The removal of North, or the whole detestable junto, is a matter unworthy the millions we have expended. A temporary stoppage of trade, was an inconvenience, which would have sufficiently balanced the repeal of all the acts complained of, had such repeals been obtained; but if the whole continent must take up arms, if every man must be a soldier, it is scarcely worth our while to fight against a contemptible ministry only. Dearly, dearly, do we pay for the repeal of the acts, if that is all we fight for; for in a just estimation, it is as great a folly to pay a Bunker-hill price for law, as for land. As I have always considered the independency of this continent, as an event, which sooner or later must arrive, so from the late rapid progress of the continent to maturity, the event could not be far off. Wherefore, on the breaking out of hostilities, it was not worth the while to have disputed a matter, which time would have finally redressed, unless we meant to be in earnest; otherwise, it is like wasting an estate on a suit at law, to regulate the trespasses of a tenant, whose lease is just expiring. No man was a warmer wisher for reconciliation than myself, before the fatal nineteenth of April 1775, but the moment the event of that day was made known, I rejected the hardened, sullen tempered Pharaoh of England for ever; and disdain the wretch, that with the pretended title of FATHER OF HIS PEOPLE, can unfeelingly hear of their slaughter, and composedly sleep with their blood upon his soul.

But admitting that matters were now made up, what would be the event? I answer, the ruin of the continent. And that for several reasons.

First. The powers of governing still remaining in the hands of the king, he will have a negative over the whole legislation of this continent. And as he hath shewn himself such an inveterate enemy to liberty, and discovered such a thirst for arbitrary power; is he, or is he not, a proper man to say to these colonies, "You shall make no laws but what I please." And is there any inhabitant in America so ignorant, as not to know, that according to what is called the present constitution, that this continent can make no laws but what the king gives it leave to; and is there any man so unwise, as not to see, that (considering what has happened) he will suffer no law to be made here, but such as suit his purpose. We may be as effectually enslaved by the want of laws in America, as by submitting to laws made for us in England. After matters are made up (as it is called) can there be any doubt, but the whole power of the crown will be exerted, to keep this continent as low and humble as possible? Instead of going forward we shall go backward, or be perpetually quarrelling or ridiculously petitioning.—We are

This painting is a romanticized depiction of the Sons of Liberty destroying a King George III statue after the Declaration was read by George Washington. Painted by Johannes Oentel, 1859.

already greater than the king wishes us to be, and will he not hereafter endeavour to make us less? To bring the matter to one point. Is the power who is jealous of our prosperity, a proper power to govern us? Whoever says No to this question is an independent, for independency means no more, than, whether we shall make our own laws, or, whether the king, the greatest enemy this continent hath, or can have, shall tell us, "there shall be no laws but such as I like."

But the king you will say has a negative in England; the people there can make no laws without his consent. In point of right and good order, there is something very ridiculous, that a youth of twenty-one (which hath often happened) shall say to several millions of people, older and wiser than himself, I forbid this or that act of yours to be law. But in this place I decline this sort of reply, though I will never cease to expose the absurdity of it, and only answer, that England being the King's residence, and America not so, make quite another case. The king's negative here is ten times more dangerous and fatal than it can be in England, for there he will scarcely refuse his consent to a bill for putting England into as strong a state of defence as possible, and in America he would never suffer such a bill to be passed.

America is only a secondary object in the system of British politics. England consults the good of this country, no farther than it answers her own purpose. Wherefore, her own interest leads her to suppress the growth of ours in every case which doth not promote her advantage, or in the least interferes with it. A pretty state we should soon be in under such a second-hand government, considering what has happened! Men do not change from enemies to friends by the alteration of a name: And in order to shew that reconciliation now is a dangerous doctrine, I affirm, that it would be policy in the king at this time, to repeal the acts for the sake of reinstating himself in the government of the provinces; in order that HE MAY ACCOMPLISH BY CRAFT AND SUBTILITY, IN THE LONG RUN, WHAT HE CANNOT DO BY FORCE AND VIOLENCE IN THE SHORT ONE. Reconciliation and ruin are nearly related.

Secondly. That as even the best terms, which we can expect to obtain, can amount to no more than a temporary expedient, or a kind of government by guardianship, which can last no longer than till the colonies come of age, so the general face and state of things, in the interim, will be unsettled and unpromising. Emigrants of property will not choose to come to a country whose form of government hangs but by a thread, and who is every day tottering on the brink of commotion and disturbance; and numbers of the present inhabitants would lay hold of the interval, to dispose of their effects, and quit the continent.

But the most powerful of all arguments, is, that nothing but independence, i.e. a continental form of government, can keep the peace of the continent and preserve it inviolate from civil wars. I dread the event of a reconciliation with Britain now, as it is more than probable, that it will be followed by a revolt somewhere or other, the consequences of which may be far more fatal than all the malice of Britain.

Thousands are already ruined by British barbarity; (thousands more will probably suffer the same fate.) Those men have other feelings than us who have nothing suffered. All they now possess is liberty, what they before enjoyed is sacrificed to its service, and having nothing more to lose, they disdain submission. Besides, the general temper of the colonies, towards a British government, will be like that of a youth, who is nearly out of his time; they will care very little about her. And a government which cannot preserve the peace, is no government at all, and in that case we pay our money for nothing; and pray what is it that Britain can do, whose power will be wholly on paper, should a civil tumult break out the very day after reconciliation? I have heard some men say,

House of Commons, 1770s

many of whom I believe spoke without thinking, that they dreaded an independence, fearing that it would produce civil wars. It is but seldom that our first thoughts are truly correct, and that is the case here; for there are ten times more to dread from a patched up connexion than from independence. I make the sufferers, case my own, and I protest, that were I driven from house and home, my property destroyed, and my circumstances ruined, that as a man, sensible of injuries, I could never relish the doctrine of reconciliation, or consider myself bound thereby.

The colonies have manifested such a spirit of good order and obedience to continental government, as is sufficient to make every reasonable person easy and happy on that head. No man can assign the least pretence for his fears, on any other grounds, that such as are truly childish and ridiculous, viz. that one colony will be striving for superiority over another.

Where there are no distinctions there can be no superiority, perfect equality affords no temptation. The republics of Europe are all (and we may say always) in peace. Holland and Swisserland are without wars, foreign or domestic: Monarchical governments, it is true, are never long at rest; the crown itself is a temptation to enterprizing ruffians at home; and that degree of pride and insolence ever attendant on regal authority, swells into a rupture with foreign powers, in instances, where a republican government, by being formed on more natural principles, would negotiate the mistake.

If there is any true cause of fear respecting independence, it is because no plan is yet laid down. Men do not see their way out— Wherefore, as an opening into that business, I offer the following hints; at the same time modestly affirming, that I have no other opinion of them myself, than that they may be the means of giving rise to something better. Could the straggling thoughts of individuals be collected, they would frequently form materials for wise and able men to improve into useful matter.

Let the assemblies be annual, with a President only. The representation more equal. Their business wholly domestic, and subject to the authority of a Continental Congress.

Let each colony be divided into six, eight, or ten, convenient districts, each district to send a proper number of delegates to Congress, so that each colony send at least thirty. The whole number in Congress will be least 390. Each Congress to sit and to choose a president by the following method. When the delegates are met, let a colony be taken from the whole thirteen colonies by lot, after which, let the whole Congress choose (by ballot) a president from out of the delegates of that province. In the next Congress, let a colony be taken by lot from twelve only, omitting that colony from which the president was taken in the former Congress, and so proceeding on till the whole thirteen shall have had their proper rotation. And in order that nothing may pass into a law but what is satisfactorily just, not less than three fifths of the Congress to be called a majority.—He that will promote discord, under a government so equally formed as this, would have joined Lucifer in his revolt.

But as there is a peculiar delicacy, from whom, or in what manner, this business must first arise, and as it seems most agreeable and consistent that it should come from some intermediate body between the governed and the governors, that is, between the Congress and the people, let a CONTINENTAL CONFERENCE be held, in the following manner, and for the following purpose.

A committee of twenty-six members of Congress, viz. two for each colony. Two members for each House of Assembly, or Provincial Convention; and five representatives of the people at large, to be chosen in the capital city or town of each province, for, and in behalf of the whole province, by as many qualified voters as shall think proper to attend from all parts of the province for that purpose; or, if more convenient, the representatives may be chosen in two or three of the most populous parts thereof. In this conference, thus assembled, will be united, the two grand principles of business, knowledge and power. The members of Congress, Assemblies, or Conventions, by having had experience in national concerns, will be able and useful counsellors, and the whole, being impowered by the people, will have a truly legal authority.

The conferring members being met, let their business be to frame a CONTINENTAL CHARTER, or Charter of the United Colonies; (answering to what is called the Magna Charta of England) fixing the number and manner of choosing members of Congress, members of Assembly, with their date of sitting, and drawing the line of business and jurisdiction between them: (Always remembering, that our strength is continental, not provincial:) Securing freedom and property to all men, and above all things, the free exercise of religion, according to the dictates of conscience; with such other matter as is necessary for a charter to contain. Immediately after which, the said Conference to dissolve, and the bodies which shall be chosen comformable to the said charter, to be the legislators and governors of this continent for the time being: Whose peace and happiness, may God preserve, Amen.

Should any body of men be hereafter delegated for this or some similar purpose, I offer them the

The Magna Carta on display at Salibury Cathedral in the United Kingdom. This is one of four surviving Magna Carta documents.

following extracts from that wise observer on governments Dragonetti. "The science," says he "of the politician consists in fixing the true point of happiness and freedom. Those men would deserve the gratitude of ages, who should discover a mode of government that contained the greatest sum of individual happiness, with the least national expense." (Dragonetti on "Virtue and Rewards.")

But where say some is the King of America? I'll tell you Friend, he reigns above, and doth not make havoc of mankind like

Colored wood engraving depicting King John of England signing the Magna Carta

the Royal Brute of Britain. Yet that we may not appear to be defective even in earthly honors, let a day be solemnly set apart for proclaiming the charter; let it be brought forth placed on the divine law, the word of God; let a crown be placed thereon, by which the world may know, that so far as we approve of monarchy, that in America THE LAW IS KING. For as in absolute governments the King is law, so in free countries the law ought to be King; and there ought to be no other. But lest any ill use should afterwards arise, let the crown at the conclusion of the ceremony be demolished, and scattered among the people whose right it is.

A government of our own is our natural right: And when a man seriously reflects on the precariousness of human affairs, he will become convinced, that it is infinitely wiser and safer, to form a constitution of our own in a cool deliberate manner, while we have it in our power, than to trust such an interesting event to time and chance. If we omit it now, some Massanello may hereafter arise, who laying hold of popular disquietudes, may collect together the desperate and discontented, and by assuming to themselves the powers of government, may sweep away the liberties of the continent like a deluge. Should the government of America return again into the hands of Britain, the tottering situation of things, will be a temptation for some desperate adventurer to try his fortune; and in such a case, what relief can Britain give? Ere she could hear the news, the fatal business might be done; and ourselves suffering like the wretched Britons under the oppression of the Conqueror. Ye that oppose independence now, ye know not what ye do; ye are opening a door to eternal tyranny, by keeping vacant the seat of government. There are thousands, and tens of thousands, who would think it glorious to expel from the continent, that barbarous and hellish power, which hath stirred up the Indians and Negroes to destroy us, the cruelty hath a double guilt, it is dealing brutally by us, and treacherously by them.

To talk of friendship with those in whom our reason forbids us to have faith, and our affections wounded through a thousand pores instruct us to detest, is madness and folly. Every day wears out the little remains of kindred between us and them, and can there be any reason to hope, that as the relationship expires, the affection will increase, or that we shall agree better, when we have ten times more and greater concerns to quarrel over than ever?

Ye that tell us of harmony and reconciliation, can ye restore to us the time that is past? Can ye give to prostitution its former innocence? Neither can ye reconcile Britain and America. The last cord now is broken, the people of England are presenting addresses against us. There are injuries which nature cannot forgive; she would cease to be nature if she did. As well can the lover forgive the ravisher of his mistress, as the continent forgive the murders of Britain. The Almighty hath implanted in us these unextinguishable feelings for good and wise purposes. They are the guardians of his image in our hearts. They distinguish us from the herd of common animals. The social compact would dissolve, and justice be extirpated from the earth, or have only a casual existence were we callous to the touches of affection. The robber, and the murderer, would often escape unpunished, did not the injuries which our tempers sustain, provoke us into justice.

O ye that love mankind! Ye that dare oppose, not only the tyranny, but the tyrant, stand forth! Every spot of the old world is overrun with oppression. Freedom hath been hunted round the globe. Asia, and Africa, have long expelled her.—Europe regards her like a stranger, and England hath given her warning to depart. O! receive the fugitive, and prepare in time an asylum for mankind.

Of the Present Ability of America: With Some Miscellaneous Reflections

I HAVE never met with a man, either in England or America, who hath not confessed his opinion, that a separation between the countries would take place one time or other: And there is no instance in which we have shown less judgment, than in endeavoring to describe, what we call, the ripeness or fitness of the continent for independence.

As all men allow the measure, and vary only in their opinion of the time, let us, in order to remove mistakes, take a general survey of things, and endeavor if possible to find out the VERY time. But I need not go far, the inquiry ceases at once, for the TIME HATH FOUND US. The general concurrence, the glorious union of all things, proves the fact.

'Tis not in numbers but in unity that our great strength lies: yet our present numbers are sufficient to repel the force of all the world. The Continent hath at this time the largest body of armed and disciplined men of any power under Heaven: and is just arrived at that pitch of strength, in which no single colony is able to support itself, and the whole, when united, is able to do any thing. Our land force is more than sufficient, and as to Naval affairs, we cannot be insensible that Britain would never suffer an American man of war to be built, while the Continent remained in her hands. Wherefore, we should be no forwarder an hundred years hence in that branch than we are now; but the truth is, we should be less so, because the timber of the Country is every day diminishing, and that which will remain at last, will be far off or difficult to procure.

Were the Continent crowded with inhabitants, her sufferings under the present circumstances would be intolerable. The more seaport-towns we had, the more should we have both to defend and to lose. Our present numbers are so happily proportioned to our wants, that no man need be idle. The diminution of trade affords an army, and the necessities of an army create a new trade.

Debts we have none: and whatever we may contract on this account will serve as a glorious memento of our virtue. Can we but leave posterity with a settled form of government, an independent constitution of its own, the purchase at any price will be cheap. But to expend millions for the sake of getting a few vile acts repealed, and routing the present ministry only, is unworthy the charge, and is using posterity with the utmost cruelty; because it is leaving them the great work to do, and a debt upon their backs from which they derive no advantage. Such a thought's unworthy a man of honour, and is the true characteristic of a narrow heart and a piddling politician.

The debt we may contract doth not deserve our regard if the work be but accomplished. No nation ought to be without a debt.

A national debt is a national bond; and when it bears no interest, is in no case a grievance. Britain is oppressed with a debt of upwards of one hundred and forty millions sterling, for which she pays upwards of four millions interest. And as a compensation for her debt, she has a large navy; America is without a debt, and without a navy; yet for the twentieth part of the English national debt, could have a navy as large again. The navy of England is not worth at this time more than three millions and a half sterling.

The first and second editions of this pamphlet were published without the following calculations, which are now given as a proof that the above estimation of the navy is a just one. See Entic's "Naval History," Intro., p. 56.

The charge of building a ship of each rate, and furnishing her with masts, yards, sails, and rigging, together with a proportion of

Guns were a vital component of any country's navy. Cannons line the sides of the British and French ships in this illustration of the siege of La Rochelle. Created by artist Rouargue in 1850.

eight months boatswain's and carpenter's sea-stores, as calculated by Mr. Burchett, Secretary to the navy.

For a ship of 100 guns, ... 35,553 £

90 " 29,886

80 " 23,638

70 " 17,785

60 " 14,197

50 " 10,606

40 " 7,558

30 " 5,846

20 " 3,710

And hence it is easy to sum up the value, or cost, rather, of the whole British navy, which, in the year 1757, when it was at its greatest glory, consisted of the following ships and guns.

Ships	Guns	Cost of One	Cost of All
6	100	35,553 £	213,318 £
12	90	29,886	358,632
12	80	23,638	283,656
43	70	17,785	764,755
35	60	14,197	496,895
40	50	10,605	424,240
45	40	7,558	340,110
58	20	3,710	215,180

85 sloops, bombs, and fireships,

one with another at 2,000 . . . 170,000

Cost, ... 3,266,786 £

Remains for guns, ... 233,214

Total, ... 3,500,000 £

No country on the globe is so happily situated, or so internally capable of raising a fleet as America. Tar, timber, iron, and cordage are her natural produce. We need go abroad for nothing. Whereas the Dutch, who make large profits by hiring out their ships of war to the Spaniards and Portuguese, are obliged to import most of

Antique naval cannonballs

the materials they use. We ought to view the building a fleet as an article of commerce, it being the natural manufactory of this country. 'Tis the best money we can lay out. A navy when finished is worth more than it cost: And is that nice point in national policy, in which commerce and protection are united. Let us build; if we want them not, we can sell; and by that means replace our paper currency with ready gold and silver.

In point of manning a fleet, people in general run into great errors; it is not necessary that one-fourth part should be sailors. The Terrible privateer, captain Death, stood the hottest engagement of any ship last war, yet had not twenty sailors on board, though her complement of men was upwards of two hundred. A few able and social sailors will soon instruct a sufficient number of active landsmen in the common work of a ship. Wherefore we never can be more capable of beginning on maritime matters than now, while our timber is standing, our fisheries blocked up, and our sailors and shipwrights out of employ. Men of war, of seventy and eighty guns, were built forty years ago in New England, and why not the same now? Ship building is America's greatest pride, and in which she will, in time, excel the whole world. The great empires of the east are mainly inland, and consequently excluded from the possibility of rivalling her. Africa is in a state of barbarism; and no power in Europe hath either such an extent of coast, or such an internal supply of materials. Where nature hath given the one, she hath withheld the other; to America only hath she been liberal to both. The vast empire of Russia is almost shut out from the sea; wherefore her boundless forests, her tar, iron and cordage are only articles of commerce.

In point of safety, ought we to be without a fleet? We are not the little people now which we were sixty years ago; at that time we might have trusted our property in the streets, or fields rather, and slept securely without locks or bolts to our doors and windows. The case is now altered, and our methods of defence ought to improve with our increase of property. A common pirate, twelve months ago, might have come up the Delaware, and laid the city of Philadelphia under contribution for what sum he pleased; and the same might have happened to other places. Nay, any daring fellow, in a brig of fourteen or sixteen guns, might have robbed the whole Continent, and carried off half a million of money. These are circumstances which demand our attention, and point out the necessity of naval protection.

Some perhaps will say, that after we have made it up with Britain, she will protect us. Can they be so unwise as to mean that she will keep a navy in our harbors for that purpose? Common sense will tell us that the power which hath endeavoured to subdue us, is of all others the most improper to defend us. Conquest may be effected under the pretence of friendship; and ourselves, after a long and brave resistance, be at last cheated into slavery. And if her ships are not to be admitted into our harbours, I would ask, how is she going to protect us? A navy three or four thousand miles off can be of little use, and on sudden emergencies, none at all. Wherefore if we must hereafter protect ourselves, why not do it for ourselves? Why do it for another?

The English list of ships of war is long and formidable, but not a tenth part of them are at any time fit for service, numbers of them are not in being; yet their names are pompously continued in the list; if only a plank be left of the ship; and not a fifth part of such as are fit for service can be spared on any one station at one time. The East and West Indies, Mediterranean, Africa, and other parts, over which Britain extends her claim, make large demands upon her navy. From a mixture of prejudice and inattention we have contracted a false notion respecting the navy of England, and have talked as if we should have the whole of it to encounter at once, and for that reason supposed that we must have one as large; which not being instantly practicable, has been made use of by a set of disguised Tories to discourage our beginning thereon. Nothing can be further from truth than this; for if America had only a twentieth part of the naval force of Britain, she would be by far an over-match for her; because, as we neither have, nor claim any foreign dominion, our whole force would be employed on our own coast, where we should, in the long run, have two to one the advantage of those who had three or four thousand miles to sail over before they could attack us, and the same distance to return in order to refit and recruit. And although Britain, by her fleet, hath a check over our trade to Europe, we have as large a one over her trade to the West Indies, which, by laying in the neighborhood of the Continent, lies entirely at its mercy.

Some method might be fallen on to keep up a naval force in time of peace, if we should judge it necessary to support a constant navy. If premiums were to be given to merchants to build and employ in their service ships mounted with twenty, thirty, forty, or fifty guns (the premiums to be in proportion to the loss of bulk to the merchant), fifty or sixty of those ships, with a few guardships on constant duty, would keep up a sufficient navy, and that without burdening ourselves with the evil so loudly complained of in England, of suffering their fleet in time of peace to lie rotting in the docks. To unite the sinews of commerce and defence is sound policy; for when our strength and our riches play into each other's hand, we need fear no external enemy.

In almost every article of defence we abound. Hemp flourishes even to rankness so that we need not want cordage. Our iron is superior to that of other countries. Our small arms equal to any in the world. Cannon we can cast at pleasure. Saltpetre and gunpowder we are every day producing. Our knowledge is hourly improving. Resolution is our inherent character, and courage hath never yet forsaken us. Wherefore, what is it that we want? Why is it that we hesitate? From Britain we can expect nothing but ruin. If she is once admitted to the government of America again, this Continent will not be worth living in. Jealousies will be always arising; insurrections will be constantly happening; and who will go forth to quell them? Who will venture his life to reduce his own countrymen to a foreign obedience? The difference between Pennsylvania and Connecticut, respecting some unlocated lands, shows the insignificance of a British government, and fully proves that nothing but Continental authority can regulate Continental matters.

Another reason why the present time is preferable to all others is, that the fewer our numbers are, the more land there is yet unoccupied, which, instead of being lavished by the king on his worthless dependents, may be hereafter applied, not only to the discharge of the present debt, but to the constant support of government. No nation under Heaven hath such an advantage as this.

The infant state of the Colonies, as it is called, so far from being against, is an argument in favour of independence. We are sufficiently numerous, and were we more so we might be less united. 'Tis a matter worthy of observation that the more a country is peopled, the smaller their armies are. In military numbers, the ancients far exceeded the moderns; and the reason is evident, for trade being the consequence of population, men became too much absorbed thereby to attend to anything else. Commerce diminishes

Early map of the colonies that was printed in England

the spirit both of patriotism and military defence. And history sufficiently informs us that the bravest achievements were always accomplished in the non-age of a nation. With the increase of commerce England hath lost its spirit. The city of London, notwithstanding its numbers, submits to continued insults with the patience of a coward. The more men have to lose, the less willing are they to venture. The rich are in general slaves to fear, and submit to courtly power with the trembling duplicity of a spaniel.

Youth is the seed-time of good habits as well in nations as in individuals. It might be difficult, if not impossible, to form the Continent into one government half a century hence. The vast variety of interests, occasioned by an increase of trade and population, would create confusion. Colony would be against colony. Each being able would scorn each other's assistance; and while the proud and foolish gloried in their little distinctions the wise would lament that the union had not been formed before. Wherefore the present time is the true time for establishing it. The intimacy which is contracted in infancy, and the friendship which is formed in misfortune, are of all others the most lasting and unalterable. Our present union is marked with both these characters; we are young, and we have been distressed; but our concord hath withstood our troubles, and fixes a memorable era for posterity to glory in.

The present time, likewise, is that peculiar time which never happens to a nation but once, viz., the time of forming itself into a government. Most nations have let slip the opportunity, and by that means have been compelled to receive laws from their conquerors, instead of making laws for themselves. First, they had a king, and then a form of government; whereas the articles or charter of government should be formed first, and men delegated to execute them afterwards; but from the errors of other nations let us learn wisdom, and lay hold of the present opportunity—TO BEGIN GOVERNMENT AT THE RIGHT END.

When William the Conqueror subdued England, he gave them law at the point of the sword; and, until we consent that the seat of government in America be legally and authoritatively occupied, we shall be in danger of having it filled by some fortunate ruffian, who may treat us in the same manner, and then, where will be our freedom? Where our property?

As to religion, I hold it to be the indispensable duty of government to protect all conscientious professors thereof, and I know of no other business which government hath to do therewith. Let a man throw aside that narrowness of soul, that selfishness of principle, which the niggards of all professions are so unwilling to part with, and he will be at once delivered of his fears on that head. Suspicion is the companion of mean souls, and the bane of all good society. For myself, I fully and conscientiously believe that it is the will of the Almighty that there should be a diversity of religious opinions among us. It affords a larger field for our Christian kindness; were we all of one way of thinking, our religious dispositions would want matter for probation; and on this liberal principle I look on the various denominations among us to be like children of the same family, differing only in what is called their Christian names.

In page [59] I threw out a few thoughts on the propriety of a Continental Charter (for I only presume to offer hints, not plans) and in this place I take the liberty of re-mentioning the subject, by observing that a charter is to be understood as a bond of solemn obligation, which the whole enters into, to support the right of every separate part, whether of religion, professional freedom, or property. A firm bargain and a right reckoning make long friends.

I have heretofore likewise mentioned the necessity of a large and equal representation; and there is no political matter which more deserves our attention. A small number of electors, or a small number of representatives, are equally dangerous. But if the number of the representatives be not only small, but unequal, the danger is increased. As an instance of this, I mention the following: when the petition of the associators was before the House of Assembly of Pennsylvania, twenty-eight members only were present; all the Bucks county members, being eight, voted against it, and had seven of the Chester members done the same, this whole province had been governed by two counties only; and this danger it is always exposed to. The unwarrantable stretch likewise, which that house made in their last sitting, to gain an undue authority over the delegates of that province, ought to warn the people at large how they trust power out of their own hands. A set of instructions for their delegates were put together, which in point of sense and business would have dishonoured a school-boy, and after being approved by a few, a very few, without doors, were carried into the house, and there passed IN BEHALF OF THE WHOLE COLONY; whereas, did the whole colony know with what ill will that house had entered on some necessary public measures, they would not hesitate a moment to think them unworthy of such a trust.

Immediate necessity makes many things convenient, which if continued would grow into oppressions. Expedience and right are different things. When the calamities of America required a consultation, there was no method so ready, or at that time so proper, as to appoint persons from the several houses of assembly for that purpose; and the wisdom with which they have proceeded

American political cartoon, 1775

hath preserved this Continent from ruin. But as it is more than probable that we shall never be without a CONGRESS, every well wisher to good order must own that the mode for choosing members of that body deserves consideration. And I put it as a question to those who make a study of mankind, whether representation and election is not too great a power for one and the same body of men to possess? When we are planning for posterity, we ought to remember that virtue is not hereditary.

It is from our enemies that we often gain excellent maxims, and are frequently surprised into reason by their mistakes. Mr. Cornwall (one of the Lords of the Treasury) treated the petition of the New York Assembly with contempt, because THAT house, he said, consisted but of twenty-six members, which trifling number, he argued, could not with decency be put for the whole. We thank him for his involuntary honesty.

To CONCLUDE, however strange it may appear to some, or however unwilling they may be to think so, matters not, but many strong and striking reasons may be given to show that nothing can settle our affairs so expeditiously as an open and determined declaration for independence. Some of which are,

First.—It is the custom of Nations, when any two are at war, for some other powers, not engaged in the quarrel, to step in as mediators, and bring about the preliminaries of a peace; But while America calls herself the subject of Great Britain, no power, however well disposed she may be, can offer her mediation. Wherefore, in our present state we may quarrel on for ever.

Secondly.—It is unreasonable to suppose that France or Spain will give us any kind of assistance, if we mean only to make use of that assistance for the purpose of repairing the breach, and strengthening the connection between Britain and America; because, those powers would be sufferers by the consequences.

Thirdly.—While we profess ourselves the subjects of Britain, we must, in the eyes of foreign nations, be considered as Rebels. The precedent is somewhat dangerous to their peace, for men to be in arms under the name of subjects; we, on the spot, can solve the paradox; but to unite resistance and subjection requires an idea much too refined for common understanding.

Fourthly.—Were a manifesto to be published, and despatched to foreign Courts, setting forth the miseries we have endured, and the peaceful methods which we have ineffectually used for redress; declaring at the same time that not being able longer to live happily or safely under the cruel disposition of the British Court, we had been driven to the necessity of breaking off all connections with her; at the same time, assuring all such Courts of our peaceable disposition towards them, and of our desire of entering into trade with them; such a memorial would produce more good effects to this Continent than if a ship were freighted with petitions to Britain.

Under our present denomination of British subjects, we can neither be received nor heard abroad; the custom of all Courts is against us, and will be so, until by an independence we take rank with other nations.

These proceedings may at first seem strange and difficult, but like all other steps which we have already passed over, will in a little time become familiar and agreeable; and until an independence is declared, the Continent will feel itself like a man who continues putting off some unpleasant business from day to day, yet knows it must be done, hates to set about it, wishes it over, and is continually haunted with the thoughts of its necessity.

Appendix to The Third Edition

SINCE the publication of the first edition of this pamphlet, or rather, on the same day on which it came out, the king's speech made its appearance in this city. Had the spirit of prophecy directed the birth of this production, it could not have brought it forth at a more seasonable juncture, or at a more necessary time. The bloody-mindedness of the one, shows the necessity of pursuing the doctrine of the other. Men read by way of revenge. And the speech, instead of terrifying, prepared a way for the manly principles of independence.

Ceremony, and even silence, from whatever motives they may arise, have a hurtful tendency when they give the least degree of countenance to base and wicked performances, wherefore, if this maxim be admitted, it naturally follows, that the king's speech, as being a piece of finished villany, deserved and still deserves, a general execration, both by the Congress and the people.

Yet, as the domestic tranquillity of a nation, depends greatly on the chastity of what might properly be called NATIONAL MANNERS, it is often better to pass some things over in silent disdain, than to make use of such new methods of dislike, as might introduce the least innovation on that guardian of our peace and safety. And, perhaps, it is chiefly owing to this prudent delicacy, that the king's speech hath not before now suffered a public execution. The speech, if it may be called one, is nothing better than a wilful audacious libel against the truth, the common good, and the existence of mankind; and is a formal and pompous method of offering up human sacrifices to the pride of tyrants.

But this general massacre of mankind, is one of the privileges and the certain consequences of kings, for as nature knows them not, they know not her, and although they are beings of our own creating, they know not us, and are become the gods of their creators. The speech hath one good quality, which is, that it is not calculated to deceive, neither can we, even if we would, be deceived by it. Brutality and tyranny appear on the face of it. It leaves us at no loss: And every line convinces, even in the moment of reading, that he who hunts the woods for prey, the naked and untutored Indian, is less savage than the king of Britain. Sir John Dalrymple, the putative father of a whining jesuitical piece, fallaciously called, "The address of the people of England to the inhabitants of America," hath perhaps from a vain supposition that the people here were to be frightened at the pomp and description of a king, given (though very unwisely on his part) the real character of the present one: "But," says this writer, "if you are inclined to pay compliments to an administration, which we do not complain of (meaning the Marquis of Rockingham's at the repeal of the Stamp Act) it is very unfair in you to withhold them from that prince, by whose NOD ALONE they were permitted to do any thing." This is toryism with a witness! Here is idolatry even without a mask: And he who can calmly hear and digest such doctrine, hath forfeited his claim to rationality an apostate from the order of manhood and ought to be considered as one who hath not only given up the proper dignity of man, but sunk himself beneath the rank of animals, and contemptibly crawls through the world like a worm.

However, it matters very little now what the king of England either says or does; he hath wickedly broken through every moral and human obligation, trampled nature and conscience beneath his feet, and by a steady and constitutional spirit of insolence and cruelty procured for himself an universal hatred. It is now the interest of America to provide for herself. She hath already a large and young family, whom it is more her duty to take care of, than to be granting away her property to support a power who is become a reproach to the names of men and christians. Ye, whose office it is to watch the morals of a nation, of whatsoever sect or denomination ye are of, as well as ye who are more immediately the guardians of the public liberty, if ye wish to preserve your native country uncontaminated by European corruption, ye must in secret wish a separation. But leaving the moral part to private

reflection, I shall chiefly confine my further remarks to the following heads:

First, That it is the interest of America to be separated from Britain.

Secondly, Which is the easiest and most practicable plan, RECONCILIATION or INDEPENDENCE? with some occasional remarks.

In support of the first, I could, if I judged it proper, produce the opinion of some of the ablest and most experienced men on this continent: and whose sentiments on that head, are not yet publicly known. It is in reality a self-evident position: for no nation in a state of foreign dependence, limited in its commerce, and cramped and fettered in its legislative powers, can ever arrive

Depiction of the battle of Bunker Hill by Percy Moran, 1909

at any material eminence. America doth not yet know what opulence is; and although the progress which she hath made stands unparalleled in the history of other nations, it is but childhood compared with what she would be capable of arriving at, had she, as she ought to have, the legislative powers in her own hands. England is at this time proudly coveting what would do her no good were she to accomplish it; and the continent hesitating on a matter which will be her final ruin if neglected. It is the commerce and not the conquest of America by which England is to be benefited, and that would in a great measure continue, were the countries as independent of each other as France and Spain; because in many articles, neither can go to a better market. But it is the independence of this country on Britain or any other which is now the main and only object worthy of contention, and which, like all other truths discovered by necessity, will appear clearer and stronger every day.

First. Because it will come to that one time or other.

Secondly. Because the longer it is delayed the harder it will be to accomplish.

I have frequently amused myself both in public and private companies, with silently remarking the specious errors of those who speak without reflecting. And among the many which I have heard, the following seems the most general, viz. that had this rupture happened forty or fifty years hence, instead of now, the continent would have been more able to have shaken off the dependence. To which I reply, that our military ability, at this time, arises from the experience gained in the last war, and which in forty or fifty years' time, would be totally extinct. The continent would not, by that time, have a general, or even a military officer left; and we, or those who may succeed us, would have been as ignorant of martial matters as the ancient Indians: And this single position, closely attended to, will unanswerably prove, that the present time is preferable to all others: The argument turns thus—at the conclusion of the last war, we had experience, but wanted numbers; and forty or fifty years hence, we should have numbers, without experience; wherefore, the proper point of time, must be some particular point between the two extremes, in which a sufficiency of the former remains, and a proper increase of the latter is obtained: And that point of time is the present time.

The reader will pardon this digression, as it does not properly come under the head I first set out with, and to which I again return by the following position, viz.:

Should affairs be patched up with Britain, and she to remain the governing and sovereign power of America, (which as matters are now circumstanced, is giving up the point entirely) we shall deprive ourselves of the very means of sinking the debt we have or may contract. The value of the back lands which some of the provinces are clandestinely deprived of, by the unjust extension of the limits of Canada, valued only at five pounds sterling per hundred acres, amount to upwards of twenty-five millions, Pennsylvania currency; and the quit-rents at one penny sterling per acre, to two millions yearly.

It is by the sale of those lands that the debt may be sunk, without burden to any, and the quit-rent reserved thereon will always lessen, and in time will wholly support, the yearly expense of government. It matters not how long the debt is in paying, so that the lands when sold be applied to the discharge of it, and for the execution of which the Congress for the time being will be the continental trustees.

I proceed now to the second head, viz. Which is the easiest and most practicable plan, reconciliation or independence; with some occasional remarks.

He who takes nature for his guide, is not easily beaten out of his argument, and on that ground, I answer generally that independence being a single simple line, contained within ourselves; and reconciliation, a matter exceedingly perplexed and complicated, and in which a treacherous capricious court is to interfere, gives the answer without a doubt.

The present state of America is truly alarming to every man who is capable of reflection. Without law, without government, without any other mode of power than what is founded on, and granted by, courtesy. Held together by an unexampled occurrence of sentiment, which is nevertheless subject to change, and which every secret enemy is endeavoring to dissolve. Our present condition is, Legislation without law; wisdom without a plan; a constitution without a name; and, what is strangely astonishing, perfect independence contending for dependence. The instance is without a precedent, the case never existed before, and who can tell what may be the event? The property of no man is secure in the present un-braced system of things. The mind of the multitude is left at random, and seeing no fixed object before them, they pursue such as fancy or opinion presents. Nothing is criminal; there is no such thing as treason, wherefore, every one thinks himself at liberty to act as he pleases. The Tories would not have dared to assemble offensively, had they known that their lives, by that act, were forfeited to the laws of the state. A line of distinction should be drawn between English soldiers taken in battle, and inhabitants of America taken in arms. The first are prisoners, but the latter traitors. The one forfeits his

Artist's rendering of the midnight ride of Paul Revere, courtesy of the National Archives

liberty, the other his head.

Notwithstanding our wisdom, there is a visible feebleness in some of our proceedings which gives encouragement to dissensions. The continental belt is too loosely buckled: And if something is not done in time, it will be too late to do any thing, and we shall fall into a state, in which neither reconciliation nor independence will be practicable. The king and his worthless adherents are got at their old game of dividing the continent, and there are not wanting among us printers who will be busy in spreading specious falsehoods. The artful and hypocritical letter which appeared a few months ago in two of the New York papers, and likewise in two others, is an evidence that there are men who want both judgment and honesty.

It is easy getting into holes and corners, and talking of reconciliation: But do such men seriously consider how difficult the task is, and how dangerous it may prove, should the continent divide thereon? Do they take within their view all the various orders of men whose situation and circumstances, as well as their own, are to be considered therein? Do they put themselves in the place of the sufferer whose all is already gone, and of the soldier, who hath quitted all for the defence of his country? If their ill-judged moderation be suited to their own private situations only, regardless of others, the event will convince them that "they are reckoning without their host."

Put us, say some, on the footing we were in the year 1763: To which I answer, the request is not now in the power of Britain to comply with, neither will she propose it; but if it were, and even should be granted, I ask, as a reasonable question, By what means is such a corrupt and faithless court to be kept to its engagements? Another parliament, nay, even the present, may hereafter repeal the obligation, on the pretence of its being violently obtained, or not wisely granted; and, in that case, Where is our redress? No going to law with nations; cannon are the barristers of crowns; and the sword, not of justice, but of war, decides the suit. To be on the footing of 1763, it is not sufficient, that the laws only be put in the same state, but, that our circumstances likewise be put in the same state; our burnt and destroyed towns repaired or built up, our private losses made good, our public debts (contracted for defence) discharged; otherwise we shall be millions worse than we were at that enviable period. Such a request, had it been complied with a year ago, would have won the heart and soul of the continent, but now it is too late. "The Rubicon is passed."

Besides, the taking up arms, merely to enforce the repeal of a pecuniary law, seems as unwarrantable by the divine law, and as repugnant to human feelings, as the taking up arms to enforce obedience thereto. The object, on either side, doth not justify the means; for the lives of men are too valuable to be cast away on such trifles. It is the violence which is done and threatened to our persons; the destruction of our property by an armed force; the invasion of our country by fire and sword, which conscientiously qualifies the use of arms: and the instant in which such mode of defence became necessary, all subjection to Britain ought to have ceased; and the independence of America should have been considered as dating its era from, and published by, the first musket that was fired against her. This line is a line of consistency; neither drawn by caprice, nor extended by ambition; but produced by a chain of events, of which the colonies were not the authors.

I shall conclude these remarks, with the following timely and well-intended hints. We ought to reflect, that there are three different ways by which an independency may hereafter be effected, and that one of those three, will, one day or other, be the fate of America, viz. By the legal voice of the people in Congress; by a military power, or by a mob: It may not always happen that our soldiers are citizens, and the multitude a body of reasonable men; virtue, as I have already remarked, is not hereditary, neither is it perpetual. Should an independency be brought about by the first of those means, we have every opportunity and every encouragement before us, to form the noblest, purest constitution on the face of the earth. We have it in our power to begin the world over again. A situation, similar to the present, hath not happened since the days of Noah until now.

The birthday of a new world is at hand, and a race of men, perhaps as numerous as all Europe contains, are to receive their portion of freedom from the events of a few months. The reflection is awful, and in this point of view, how trifling, how ridiculous, do the little paltry cavilings of a few weak or interested men appear, when weighed against the business of a world.

Should we neglect the present favorable and inviting period, and independence be hereafter effected by any other means, we must charge the consequence to ourselves, or to those rather whose narrow and prejudiced souls are habitually opposing the measure, without either inquiring or reflecting. There are reasons to be given in support of independence which men should rather privately think of, than be publicly told of. We ought not now to be debating whether we shall be independent or not, but anxious to accomplish it on a firm, secure, and honorable basis, and uneasy rather that it is not yet began upon. Every day convinces us of its necessity. Even the Tories (if such beings yet remain among us) should, of all men, be the most solicitous to promote it; for as the appointment of committees at first protected them from popular rage, so, a wise and well established form of government will be the only certain means of continuing it securely to them. Wherefore, if they have not virtue enough to be WHIGS, they ought to have prudence enough to wish for independence.

In short, independence is the only bond that tie and keep us together. We shall then see our object, and our ears will be legally shut against the schemes of an intriguing, as well as cruel, enemy. We shall then, too, be on a proper footing to treat with Britain; for there is reason to conclude, that the pride of that court will be less hurt by treating with the American States for terms of peace, than with those, whom she denominates "rebellious subjects," for terms of accommodation. It is our delaying in that, encourages her to hope for conquest, and our backwardness tends only to prolong the war. As we have, without any good effect therefrom, withheld our trade to obtain a redress of our grievances, let us now try the alternative, by independently redressing them ourselves, and then offering to open the trade. The mercantile and reasonable part of England, will be still with us; because, peace, with trade, is preferable to war without it. And if this offer be not accepted, other courts may be applied to.

On these grounds I rest the matter. And as no offer hath yet been made to refute the doctrine contained in the former editions of this pamphlet, it is a negative proof, that either the doctrine cannot be refuted, or, that the party in favor of it are too numerous to be opposed. WHEREFORE, instead of gazing at each other with suspicious or doubtful curiosity, let each of us hold out to his neighbor the hearty hand of friendship, and unite in drawing a line, which, like an act of oblivion, shall bury in forgetfulness every former dissension. Let the names of Whig and Tory be extinct; and let none other be heard among us, than those of a good citizen, an open and resolute friend, and a virtuous supporter of the RIGHTS of MANKIND, and of the FREE AND INDE-PENDENT STATES OF AMERICA.

Colonial flag with stars for the 13 original colonies

THE DECLARATION OF INDEPENDENCE

★ ★ ★

*B*y the time—most notably—the cousins Samuel and John Adams of Massachusetts, Ben Franklin of Pennsylvania, and Richard Henry Lee of Virginia had complained and nudged and bullied the Second Continental Congress into taking up the issue of Independence, the war was already well under way. The battles at Lexington and Concord and Bunker Hill had already spilled much blood. George Washington, who had already been dispatched to command what people were now calling the Continental Army, had managed to force the British Army's evacuation of Boston, and was in the process of bringing his army to New York to attempt the defense of that city. The success of the Articles of Association in staving off anarchy and in providing an organizing principle for thousands of individuals in hundreds of localities throughout the colonies demonstrated a decidedly post-colonial mindset. All of these things together suggest that the spirit of "Independency" was already strong among many—if not most—of the people. As we *have seen many times since, the people were well ahead of their representatives.*

Thomas Jefferson of Virginia was chosen to draft the Declaration and he managed a workmanlike job of it, scolding the King and his ministers for every offense he could think of. However, it is with the first thirty-six words of the second paragraph, the ones beginning with "We hold these truths . . ." that Jefferson penned the most famous, the most significant words in all the literature of our history. Every person is free. Every person has certain rights. These rights are not the gift of king or government, but are held directly from God.

IN CONGRESS
JULY 4, 1776

THE DECLARATION OF INDEPENDENCE

When, in the course of human events, it becomes necessary for one people to dissolve the political bands which have connected them with another, and to assume among the powers of the earth, the separate and equal station to which the laws of nature and of nature's God entitle them, a decent respect to the opinions of mankind requires that they should declare the causes which impel them to the separation.

We hold these truths to be self-evident, that all men are created equal, that they are endowed by their Creator with certain unalienable rights, that among these are life, liberty and the pursuit of happiness. That to secure these rights, governments are instituted among men, deriving their just powers from the consent of the governed. That whenever any form of government becomes destructive to these ends, it is the right of the people to alter or to abolish it, and to institute new government, laying its foundation on such principles and organizing its powers in such form, as to them shall seem most likely to effect their safety and happiness. Prudence, indeed, will dictate that governments long established should not be changed for light and transient causes; and accordingly all experience hath shown that mankind are more disposed to suffer, while evils are sufferable, than to right themselves by abolishing the forms to which they are accustomed. But when a long train of abuses and usurpations, pursuing invariably the same object evinces a design to reduce them under absolute despotism, it is their right, it is their duty, to throw off such government, and to provide new guards for their future security.—Such has been the patient sufferance of these colonies; and such is now the necessity which constrains them to alter their former systems of government. The history of the present King of Great Britain is a history of repeated injuries and usurpations, all having in direct object the establishment of an absolute tyranny over these states. To prove this, let facts be submitted to a candid world.

He has refused his assent to laws, the most wholesome and necessary for the public good.

He has forbidden his governors to pass laws of immediate and pressing importance, unless suspended in their operation till his assent should be obtained; and when so suspended, he has utterly neglected to attend to them.

He has refused to pass other laws for the accommodation of large districts of people, unless those people would relinquish the right of representation in the legislature, a right inestimable to them and formidable to tyrants only.

Benjamin Franklin, John Adams, and Thomas Jefferson review a draft of the Declaration of Independence. The painting is by J.L.G. Ferris.

He has called together legislative bodies at places unusual, uncomfortable, and distant from the depository of their public records, for the sole purpose of fatiguing them into compliance with his measures.

He has dissolved representative houses repeatedly, for opposing with manly firmness his invasions on the rights of the people.

He has refused for a long time, after such dissolutions, to cause others to be elected; whereby the legislative powers, incapable of annihilation, have returned to the people at large for their exercise; the state remaining in the meantime exposed to all the dangers of invasion from without, and convulsions within.

He has endeavored to prevent the population of these states; for that purpose obstructing the laws for naturalization of foreigners; refusing to pass others to encourage their migration hither, and raising the conditions of new appropriations of lands.

He has obstructed the administration of justice, by refusing his assent to laws for establishing judiciary powers.

He has made judges dependent on his will alone, for the tenure of their offices, and the amount and payment of their salaries.

He has erected a multitude of new offices, and sent hither swarms of officers to harass our people, and eat out their substance.

He has kept among us, in times of peace, standing armies without the consent of our legislature.

Samuel Adams

John Trumbull's painting, The Declaration of Independence, *depicting the five-man drafting committee of the Declaration of Independence presenting their work to Congress.*

He has affected to render the military independent of and superior to civil power.

He has combined with others to subject us to a jurisdiction foreign to our constitution, and unacknowledged by our laws; giving his assent to their acts of pretended legislation:

For quartering large bodies of armed troops among us:

For protecting them, by mock trial, from punishment for any murders which they should commit on the inhabitants of these states:

For cutting off our trade with all parts of the world:

For imposing taxes on us without our consent:

For depriving us in many cases, of the benefits of trial by jury:

For transporting us beyond seas to be tried for pretended offenses:

For abolishing the free system of English laws in a neighboring province, establishing therein an arbitrary government, and enlarging its boundaries so as to render it at once an example and fit instrument for introducing the same absolute rule in these colonies:

For taking away our charters, abolishing our most valuable laws, and altering fundamentally the forms of our governments:

For suspending our own legislatures, and declaring themselves invested with power to legislate for us in all cases whatsoever.

He has abdicated government here, by declaring us out of his protection and waging war against us.

He has plundered our seas, ravaged our coasts, burned our towns, and destroyed the lives of our people.

He is at this time transporting large armies of foreign mercenaries to complete the works of death, desolation and tyranny, already begun with circumstances of cruelty and perfidy scarcely paralleled in the most barbarous ages, and totally unworthy the head of a civilized nation.

He has constrained our fellow citizens taken captive on the high seas to bear arms against their country, to become the executioners of their friends and brethren, or to fall themselves by their hands.

He has excited domestic insurrections amongst us, and has endeavored to bring on the inhabitants of our frontiers, the merciless Indian savages, whose known rule of warfare, is undistinguished destruction of all ages, sexes and conditions.

In every stage of these oppressions we have petitioned for redress in the most humble terms: our repeated petitions have been answered only by repeated injury. A prince, whose character is thus marked by every act which may define a tyrant, is unfit to be the ruler of a free people.

Nor have we been wanting in attention to our British brethren. We have warned them from time to time of attempts by their legislature to extend an unwarrantable jurisdiction over us. We have reminded them of the circumstances of our emigration and settlement here. We have appealed to their native justice and magnanimity, and we have conjured them by the ties of our common kindred to disavow these usurpations, which, would inevitably interrupt our connections and correspondence. They too have been deaf to the voice of justice and of consanguinity. We must, therefore, acquiesce in the necessity, which denounces our separation, and hold them, as we hold the rest of mankind, enemies in war, in peace friends.

We, therefore, the representatives of the United States of America, in General Congress, assembled, appealing to the Supreme Judge of the world for the rectitude of our intentions, do, in the name, and by the authority of the good people of these colonies, solemnly publish and declare, that these united colonies are, and of right ought to be free

The Declaration read aloud to colonial citizens

and independent states; that they are absolved from all allegiance to the British Crown, and that all political connection between them and the state of Great Britain, is and ought to be totally dissolved; and that as free and independent states, they have full power to levy war, conclude peace, contract alliances, establish commerce, and to do all other acts and things which independent states may of right do. And for the support of this declaration, with a firm reliance on the protection of Divine Providence, we mutually pledge to each other our lives, our fortunes and our sacred honor.

New Hampshire: Josiah Bartlett, William Whipple, Matthew Thornton

Massachusetts: John Hancock, Samual Adams, John Adams, Robert Treat Paine, Elbridge Gerry

Rhode Island: Stephen Hopkins, William Ellery

Connecticut: Roger Sherman, Samuel Huntington, William Williams, Oliver Wolcott

New York: William Floyd, Philip Livingston, Francis Lewis, Lewis Morris

New Jersey: Richard Stockton, John Witherspoon, Francis Hopkinson, John Hart, Abraham Clark

Pennsylvania: Robert Morris, Benjamin Rush, Benjamin Franklin, John Morton, George Clymer, James Smith, George Taylor, James Wilson, George Ross

Delaware: Caesar Rodney, George Read, Thomas McKean

Maryland: Samuel Chase, William Paca, Thomas Stone, Charles Carroll of Carrollton

Virginia: George Wythe, Richard Henry Lee, Thomas Jefferson, Benjamin Harrison, Thomas Nelson, Jr., Francis Lightfoot Lee, Carter Braxton

North Carolina: William Hooper, Joseph Hewes, John Penn

South Carolina: Edward Rutledge, Thomas Heyward, Jr., Thomas Lynch, Jr., Arthur Middleton

Georgia: Button Gwinnett, Lyman Hall, George Walton

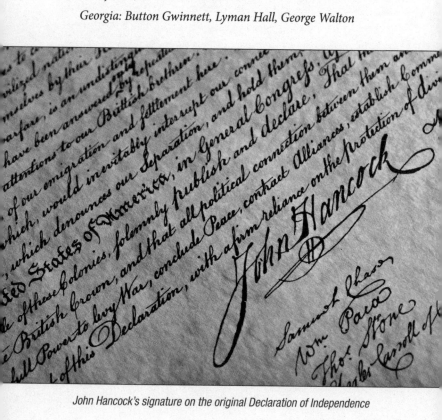

John Hancock's signature on the original Declaration of Independence

THE ARTICLES OF CONFEDERATION

★ ★ ★

The Articles of Confederation served as a working agreement between the former Colonies—now States. It was a loose arrangement whereby sovereignty was held in each State, rather than in a central or Federal government. This system didn't work very well, but it was the first draft or plan of government for what would soon become the United States of America.

Agreed to by Congress November 15, 1777; ratified and in force, March 1, 1781.

THE ARTICLES OF CONFEDERATION

PREAMBLE

To all to whom these Presents shall come, we the undersigned Delegates of the States affixed to our Names send greeting.

Whereas the Delegates of the United States of America in Congress assembled did on the fifteenth day of November in the Year of our Lord One Thousand Seven Hundred and Seventy seven, and in the Second Year of the Independence of America, agree to certain articles of Confederation and perpetual Union between the States of New Hampshire, Massachusetts-bay, Rhode Island and Providence Plantations, Connecticut, New York, New Jersey, Pennsylvania, Delaware, Maryland, Virginia, North Carolina, South Carolina and Georgia, in the words following, viz:

Articles of Confederation and perpetual Union between the States of New Hampshire, Massachusetts-bay, Rhode Island and Providence Plantations, Connecticut, New York, New Jersey, Pennsylvania, Delaware, Maryland, Virginia, North Carolina, South Carolina and Georgia.

Article I. The Stile of this Confederacy shall be "The United States of America."

Article II. Each state retains its sovereignty, freedom, and independence, and every Power, Jurisdiction, and right, which is not by this confederation expressly delegated to the United States, in Congress assembled.

Article III. The said States hereby severally enter into a firm league of friendship with each other, for their common defense, the security of their liberties, and their mutual and general welfare, binding themselves to assist each other, against all force offered to, or attacks made upon them, or any of them, on account of religion, sovereignty, trade, or any other pretense whatever.

Article IV. The better to secure and perpetuate mutual friendship and intercourse among the people of the different States in this union, the free inhabitants of each of these States, paupers, vagabonds, and fugitives from justice excepted, shall be entitled to all privileges and immunities of free citizens in the several States; and the people of each State shall have free ingress and regress to and from any other State, and shall enjoy therein all the privileges of trade and commerce, subject to the same duties, impositions, and restrictions as the inhabitants thereof respectively, provided that such restrictions shall not extend so far as to prevent the removal of property imported into any State, to any other State, of which the owner is an inhabitant; provided also that no imposition, duties or restriction shall be laid by any State, on the property of the united States, or either of them.

If any person guilty of, or charged with, treason, felony, or other high misdemeanor in any State, shall flee from justice, and be found in any of the united States, he shall, upon demand of the Governor or executive power of the State from which he fled, be delivered up and removed to the State having jurisdiction of his offense.

Full faith and credit shall be given in each of these States to the records, acts, and judicial proceedings of the courts and magistrates of every other State.

Article V. For the most convenient management of the general interests of the united States, delegates shall be annually appointed in such manner as the legislatures of each State shall direct, to meet in Congress on the first Monday in November, in every year, with a power reserved to each State to recall its delegates, or any of them, at any time within the year, and to send others in their stead for the remainder of the year.

No State shall be represented in Congress by less than two, nor more than seven members; and no person shall be capable of being a delegate for more than three years in any term of six years; nor shall any person, being a delegate, be capable of holding any office under the united States, for which he, or another for his benefit, receives any salary, fees or emolument of any kind.

Each State shall maintain its own delegates in a meeting of the States, and while they act as members of the committee of the States.

An American Soldier.
1778

Depiction of an American soldier from the Revolutionary War

In determining questions in the united States, in Congress assembled, each State shall have one vote.

Freedom of speech and debate in Congress shall not be impeached or questioned in any court or place out of Congress, and the members of Congress shall be protected in their persons from arrests or imprisonments, during the time of their going to and from, and attendance on Congress, except for treason, felony, or breach of the peace.

Article VI. No State, without the consent of the united States in Congress assembled, shall send any embassy to, or receive any embassy from, or enter into any conference, agreement, alliance or treaty with any King, Prince or State; nor shall any person holding any office of profit or trust under the united States, or any of them, accept any present, emolument, office or title of any kind whatever from any King, Prince or foreign State; nor shall the United States in congress assembled, or any of them, grant any title of nobility.

No two or more States shall enter into any treaty, confederation or alliance whatever between them, without the consent of the united States in congress assembled, specifying accurately the purposes for which the same is to be entered into, and how long it shall continue.

No State shall lay any imposts or duties, which may interfere with any stipulations in treaties, entered into by the united States in congress assembled, with any King, Prince or State, in pursuance of any treaties already proposed by congress, to the courts of France and Spain.

No vessel of war shall be kept up in time of peace by any State, except such number only, as shall be deemed necessary by the united States in congress assembled, for the defense of such State, or its trade; nor shall any body of forces be kept up by any State in time of peace, except such number only, as in the judgement of the united States, in congress assembled, shall be deemed requisite to garrison the forts necessary for the defense of such State; but every State shall always keep up a well-regulated and disciplined militia, sufficiently armed and accoutered, and shall provide and constantly have ready for use, in public stores, a due number of field pieces and tents, and a proper quantity of arms, ammunition and camp equipage.

No State shall engage in any war without the consent of the united States in congress assembled, unless such State be actually invaded by enemies, or shall have received certain advice of a resolution being formed by some nation of Indians to invade such State, and the danger is so imminent as not to admit of a delay till the united States in congress assembled can be consulted; nor shall any State grant commissions to any ships or vessels of war, nor letters of marque or reprisal, except it be after a declaration of war

Vintage stamp depicting the drafting of the Articles of Confederation

by the united States in congress assembled, and then only against the kingdom or State and the subjects thereof, against which war has been so declared, and under such regulations as shall be established by the united States in congress assembled, unless such State be infested by pirates, in which case vessels of war may be fitted out for that occasion, and kept so long as the danger shall continue, or until the united States in congress assembled shall determine otherwise.

Article VII. When land forces are raised by any State for the common defense, all officers of or under the rank of colonel, shall be appointed by the legislature of each State respectively, by whom such forces shall be raised, or in such manner as such State shall direct, and all vacancies shall be filled up by the State which first made the appointment.

Article VIII. All charges of war, and all other expenses that shall be incurred for the common defense or general welfare, and allowed by the united States in congress assembled, shall be defrayed out of a common treasury, which shall be supplied by the several States in proportion to the value of all land within each State, granted or surveyed for any person, as such land and the buildings and improvements thereon shall be estimated according to such mode as the united States in congress assembled, shall from time to time direct and appoint.

The taxes for paying that proportion shall be laid and levied by the authority and direction of the legislatures of the several States within the time agreed upon by the united States in congress assembled.

Article IX. The united States in congress assembled, shall have the sole and exclusive right and power of determining on peace and war, except in the cases mentioned in the sixth article—of sending and receiving ambassadors—entering into treaties and alliances, provided that no treaty of commerce shall be made whereby the legislative power of the respective States shall be restrained from imposing such imposts and duties on foreigners, as their own people are subjected to, or from prohibiting the exportation or importation of any species of goods or commodities whatsoever—of establishing rules for deciding in all cases, what captures on land or water shall be legal, and in what manner prizes taken by land or naval forces in the service of the United States shall be divided or appropriated—of granting letters of marque and reprisal in times of peace—appointing courts for the trial of piracies and felonies committed on the high seas and establishing courts for receiving and determining finally appeals in all cases of captures, provided that no member of Congress shall be appointed a judge of any of the said courts.

The United States in Congress assembled shall also be the last resort on appeal in all disputes and differences now subsisting or that hereafter may arise between two or more States concerning boundary, jurisdiction or any other causes whatever; which authority shall always be exercised in the manner following. Whenever the legislative or executive authority or lawful agent of any State in controversy with another shall present a petition to Congress stating the matter in question and praying for a hearing, notice thereof shall be given by order of Congress to the legislative or executive authority of the other State in controversy, and a day assigned for the appearance of the parties by their lawful agents, who shall then be directed to appoint by joint consent, commissioners or judges to constitute a court for hearing and determining the matter in question: but if they cannot agree, Congress shall name three persons out of each of the United States, and from the list of such persons each party shall alternately strike out one, the petitioners beginning, until the number shall be reduced to thirteen; and from that number not less than seven, nor more than nine names as Congress shall direct, shall in the presence of Congress be drawn out by lot, and the persons whose names shall be so drawn or any five of them, shall be commissioners or judges, to hear and finally determine the controversy, so always as a major part of the judges who shall hear the cause shall agree in the determination: and if either party shall neglect to attend at the day appointed, without showing reasons, which Congress shall judge sufficient, or being present shall refuse to strike, the Congress shall proceed to nominate three persons out of each State, and the secretary of Congress shall strike in behalf of such party absent or refusing; and the judgement and sentence of the court to be appointed, in the manner before prescribed, shall be final and conclusive; and if any of the parties shall refuse to submit to the authority of such court, or to appear or defend their claim or cause, the court shall nevertheless proceed to pronounce sentence, or judgement, which shall in like manner be final and decisive, the judgement or sentence and other proceedings being in either case transmitted to Congress, and lodged among the acts of Congress for the security of the parties concerned: provided that every commissioner, before he sits in judgement, shall take an oath to be administered by one of the judges of the supreme or superior court of the State, where the cause shall be tried, 'well and truly to hear and determine the matter in question, according to the best of his judgement, without favor, affection or hope of reward': provided also, that no State shall be deprived of territory for the benefit of the United States.

All controversies concerning the private right of soil claimed under different grants of two or more States, whose jurisdictions as they may respect such lands, and the States which passed such grants are adjusted, the said grants or either of them being at the same time claimed to have originated antecedent to such settlement of jurisdiction, shall on the petition of either party to the Congress of the United States, be finally determined as near as may be in the same manner as is before prescribed for deciding disputes respecting territorial jurisdiction between different States.

The United States in Congress assembled shall also have the sole and exclusive right and power of regulating the alloy and value of coin struck by their own authority, or by that of the respective States—fixing the standards of weights and measures throughout the United States—regulating the trade and managing all affairs with the Indians, not members of any of the States, provided that the legislative right of any State within its own limits be not infringed or violated—establishing or regulating post offices from one State to another, throughout all the United States, and exacting such postage on the papers passing through the same as may be requisite to defray the expenses of the said office—appointing all officers of the land forces, in the service of the United States, excepting regimental officers—appointing all the officers of the naval forces, and commissioning all officers whatever in the service of the United States—making rules for the government and regulation of the said land and naval forces, and directing their operations.

The United States in Congress assembled shall have authority to appoint a committee, to sit in the recess of Congress, to be denominated 'A Committee of the States', and to consist of one delegate from each State; and to appoint such other committees

The British surrender at Yorktown

and civil officers as may be necessary for managing the general affairs of the United States under their direction—to appoint one of their members to preside, provided that no person be allowed to serve in the office of president more than one year in any term of three years; to ascertain the necessary sums of money to be raised for the service of the United States, and to appropriate and apply the same for defraying the public expenses—to borrow money, or emit bills on the credit of the United States, transmitting every half-year to the respective States an account of the sums of money so borrowed or emitted—to build and equip a navy—to agree upon the number of land forces, and to make requisitions from each State for its quota, in proportion to the number of white inhabitants in such State; which requisition shall be binding, and thereupon the legislature of each State shall appoint the regimental officers, raise the men and cloath, arm and equip them in a solid—like manner, at the expense of the United States; and the officers and men so cloathed, armed and equipped shall march to the place appointed, and within the time agreed on by the United States in Congress assembled. But if the United States in Congress assembled shall, on consideration of circumstances judge proper that any State should not raise men, or should raise a smaller number of men than the quota thereof, such extra number shall be raised, officered, cloathed, armed and equipped in the same manner as the quota of each State, unless the legislature of such State shall judge that such extra number cannot be safely spread out in the same, in which case they shall raise, officer, cloath, arm and equip as many of such extra number as they judge can be safely spared. And the officers and men so cloathed, armed, and equipped, shall march to the place appointed, and within the time agreed on by the united States in congress assembled.

The united States in congress assembled shall never engage in a war, nor grant letters of marque or reprisal in time of peace, nor enter into any treaties or alliances, nor coin money, nor regulate the value thereof, nor ascertain the sums and expenses necessary for the defense and welfare of the United States, or any of them, nor emit bills, nor borrow money on the credit of the united States, nor appropriate money, nor agree upon the number of vessels of war, to be built or purchased, or the number of land or sea forces to be raised, nor appoint a commander in chief of the army or

John Hancock, as depicted by painter John Singleton Copley, 1765

navy, unless nine States assent to the same: nor shall a question on any other point, except for adjourning from day to day be determined, unless by the votes of the majority of the united States in congress assembled.

The congress of the united States shall have power to adjourn to any time within the year, and to any place within the united States, so that no period of adjournment be for a longer duration than the space of six months, and shall publish the journal of their proceedings monthly, except such parts thereof relating to treaties, alliances or military operations, as in their judgement require secrecy; and the yeas and nays of the delegates of each State on any question shall be entered on the journal, when it is desired by any delegates of a State, or any of them, at his or their request shall be furnished with a transcript of the said journal, except such parts as are above excepted, to lay before the legislatures of the several States.

Article X. The committee of the States, or any nine of them, shall be authorized to execute, in the recess of congress, such of the powers of congress as the united States in congress assembled, by the consent of the nine States, shall from time to time think expedient to vest them with; provided that no power be delegated to the said Committee, for the exercise of which, by the articles of confederation, the voice of nine States in the Congress of the United States assembled be requisite.

Article XI. Canada acceding to this confederation, and adjoining in the measures of the united States, shall be admitted into, and entitled to all the advantages of this union; but no other colony shall be admitted into the same, unless such admission be agreed to by nine States.

Article XII. All bills of credit emitted, monies borrowed, and debts contracted by, or under the authority of congress, before the assembling of the united States, in pursuance of the present confederation, shall be deemed and considered as a charge against the United States, for payment and satisfaction whereof the said united States, and the public faith are hereby solemnly pledged.

Article XIII. Every State shall abide by the determination of the united States in congress assembled, on all questions which by this confederation are submitted to them. And the Articles of this confederation shall be inviolably observed by every State, and the union shall be perpetual; nor shall any alteration at any time hereafter be made in any of them; unless such alteration be agreed to in a congress of the united States, and be afterwards confirmed by the legislatures of every State.

And Whereas it hath pleased the Great Governor of the World to incline the hearts of the legislatures we respectively represent in Congress, to approve of, and to authorize us to ratify the said articles of confederation and perpetual union. Know Ye that we the undersigned delegates, by virtue of the power and authority to us given for that purpose, do by these presents, in the name and in behalf of our respective constituents, fully and entirely ratify and confirm each and every of the said articles of confederation and perpetual union, and all and singular the matters and things therein contained: And we do further solemnly plight and engage the faith of our respective constituents, that they shall abide by the determi-

Independence Hall, 1752

nations of the united States in congress assembled, on all questions, which by the said confederation are submitted to them. And that the articles thereof shall be inviolably observed by the States we respectively represent, and that the union shall be perpetual.

In Witness whereof we have hereunto set our hands in Congress. Done at Philadelphia in the State of Pennsylvania the ninth Day of July in the Year of our Lord one thousand seven Hundred and Seventy-eight, and in the Third Year of the independence of America.

On the part and behalf of the State of New Hampshire: Josiah Bartlett, John Wentworth Junr. August 8th 1778

On the part and behalf of The State of Massachusetts Bay: John Hancock, Samuel Adams, Elbridge Gerry, Francis Dana, James Lovell, Samuel Holten

On the part and behalf of the State of Rhode Island and Providence Plantations: William Ellery, Henry Marchant, John Collins

On the part and behalf of the State of Connecticut: Roger Sherman, Samuel Huntington, Oliver Wolcott, Titus Hosmer, Andrew Adams

On the Part and Behalf of the State of New York: James Duane, Francis Lewis, Wm. Duer, Gouv Morris

On the Part and in Behalf of the State of New Jersey, November 26, 1778, Jno Witherspoon, Nath. Scudder

On the part and behalf of the State of Pennsylvania: Robt Morris, Daniel Roberdeau, John Bayard Smith, William Clingan, Joseph Reed, 22nd July 1778

On the part and behalf of the State of Delaware: Tho Mckean, February 12, 1779, John Dickinson, May 5th 1779, Nicholas Van Dyke

On the part and behalf of the State of Maryland: John Hanson, March 1 1781, Daniel Carroll

On the Part and Behalf of the State of Virginia: Richard Henry Lee, John Banister, Thomas Adams, Jno Harvie Francis, Lightfoot Lee

On the part and Behalf of the State of No Carolina: John Penn, July 21st 1778, Corns Harnett, Jno Williams

On the part and behalf of the State of South Carolina: Henry Laurens, William Henry Drayton, Jno Mathews, Richd Hutson, Thos Heyward Junr

On the part and behalf of the State of Georgia: Jno Walton 24th July 1778, Edwd Telfair, Edwd Langworthy

THE U.S. CONSTITUTION

* * *

*B*y war's end it was clear to many Americans that the Articles of Confederation did not provide a government, either sufficient or able to meet the challenges of nationhood. In the few years immediately following, people from all over the former Colonies began to call for a meeting or congress or convention to address these challenges. The result was the Philadelphia Convention of 1787. Its original mandate was to merely suggest adjustments to the Articles of Confederation. But once work began, the majority agreed that what was needed was a brand new, written Constitution.

Vintage engraving of cracked Liberty Bell from the Trousset Encyclopedia

Though Gouverneur Morris of Pennsylvania is generally credited with the drafting of the document, many historians regard James Madison as the "Father of the Constitution," —which may be overstating it.

However, Madison did help organize the Convention, and he coaxed George Washington into attending, thus guaranteeing that people would take the effort seriously. More than that, Madison came to Philadelphia armed with a plan for a Federal Government. This set of proposals, largely based upon his earlier work on the Virginia State Constitution, set the agenda for the Convention, and went a long way towards clarifying the issues on which the debates were to be joined.

Throughout the summer of 1787 these debates continued as interests, needs, prejudices and traditions were balanced, one against another. The result would be a Constitution that no one was completely happy with, but which most Americans could support. After ratification by the Philadelphia Convention, then began the process of ratification by the States. For the next two years the debate raged in newspapers and in pamphlets, in State Houses and in town meetings. Eventually, one by one, the States joined in Union. The final sticking-point was the question of the inclusion of a Bill of Rights to protect the individual from abuse of power by this new Federal Government. Madison and the Federalists considered it unnecessary, but agreed to support a Bill of Rights as the first Amendments to the Constitution.

THE CONSTITUTION OF THE UNITED STATES

We the People of the United States, in Order to form a more perfect Union, establish Justice, insure domestic Tranquility, provide for the common defense, promote the general Welfare, and secure the Blessings of Liberty to ourselves and our Posterity, do ordain and establish this Constitution for the United States of America.

ARTICLE I—LEGISLATIVE BRANCH

Section 1.—The Legislative

All legislative powers herein granted shall be vested in a Congress of the United States, which shall consist of a Senate and House of Representatives.

Section 2.—The House

The House of Representatives shall be composed of members chosen every second year by the people of the several states, and the electors in each state shall have the qualifications requisite for electors of the most numerous branch of the state legislature.

No person shall be a Representative who shall not have attained to the age of twenty five years, and been seven years a citizen of the United States, and who shall not, when elected, be an inhabitant of that state in which he shall be chosen.

(The following changed by Section 2 of the 14th Amendment)

Representatives and direct taxes shall be apportioned among the several states which may be included within this union, according to their respective numbers, which shall be determined by adding to the whole number of free persons, including those bound to service for a term of years, and excluding Indians not taxed, three fifths of all other Persons. The actual Enumeration shall be made within three years after the first meeting of the Congress of the United States, and within every subsequent term of ten years, in such manner as they shall by law direct. The number of Representatives shall not exceed one for every thirty thousand, but each state shall have at least one Representative; and until such enumeration shall be made, the state of New Hampshire shall be entitled to chuse three, Massachusetts eight, Rhode Island and Providence Plantations one, Connecticut five, New York six, New Jersey four, Pennsylvania eight, Delaware one, Maryland six, Virginia ten, North Carolina five, South Carolina five, and Georgia three.

When vacancies happen in the Representation from any state, the executive authority thereof shall issue writs of election to fill such vacancies.

The House of Representatives shall choose their speaker and other officers; and shall have the sole power of impeachment.

Section 3.—The Senate

The Senate of the United States shall be composed of two Senators from each state,

(The following superceded by the 17th Amendment)

chosen by the legislature thereof, for six years; and each Senator shall have one vote.

Immediately after they shall be assembled in consequence of the first election, they shall be divided as equally as may be into three classes. The seats of the Senators of the first class shall be vacated at the expiration of the second year, of the second class at the expiration of the fourth year, and the third class at the expiration of the sixth year, so that one third may be chosen every second year;

(Also superseded by the 17th Amendment)

and if vacancies happen by resignation, or otherwise, during the recess of the legislature of any state, the executive thereof may make temporary appointments until the next meeting of the legis-

Charles Wilson Peale's wash drawing of the Pennsylvania State House. Here the Declaration of Independence was signed, and the Constitution was framed.

lature, which shall then fill such vacancies.

No person shall be a Senator who shall not have attained to the age of thirty years, and been nine years a citizen of the United States and who shall not, when elected, be an inhabitant of that state for which he shall be chosen.

The Vice President of the United States shall be President of the Senate, but shall have no vote, unless they be equally divided.

The Senate shall choose their other officers, and also a President pro tempore, in the absence of the Vice President, or when he shall exercise the office of President of the United States.

The Senate shall have the sole power to try all impeachments. When sitting for that purpose, they shall be on oath or affirmation. When the President of the United States is tried, the Chief Justice shall preside: And no person shall be convicted without the concurrence of two thirds of the members present.

Judgment in cases of impeachment shall not extend further than to removal from office, and disqualification to hold and enjoy any office of honor, trust or profit under the United States: but the party convicted shall nevertheless be liable and subject to indictment, trial, judgment and punishment, according to law.

Section 4.—Elections, Meetings

The times, places and manner of holding elections for Senators and Representatives, shall be prescribed in each state by the legislature thereof; but the Congress may at any time by law make or alter such regulations, except as to the places of choosing Senators.

The Congress shall assemble at least once in every year, and such meeting

(The following superseded by Section 2 of the 20th Amendment)

shall be on the first Monday in December, unless they shall by law appoint a different day.

Section 5.—Membership, Rules, Journals, Adjournment

Each House shall be the judge of the elections, returns and qualifications of its own members, and a majority of each shall constitute a quorum to do business; but a smaller number may adjourn from day to day, and may be authorized to compel the attendance of absent members, in such manner, and under such penalties as each House may provide.

Each House may determine the rules of its proceedings, punish its members for disorderly behavior, and, with the concurrence of two thirds, expel a member.

Each House shall keep a journal of its proceedings, and from time to time publish the same, excepting such parts as may in their judgment require secrecy; and the yeas and nays of the members of either House on any question shall, at the desire of one fifth of those present, be entered on the journal.

Neither House, during the session of Congress, shall, without the consent of the other, adjourn for more than three days, nor to any other place than that in which the two Houses shall be sitting.

Section 6.—Compensation

(The following words are modified by the 27th Amendment)

The Senators and Representatives shall receive a compensation for their services, to be ascertained by law, and paid out of the treasury of the United States. They shall in all cases, except treason, felony and breach of the peace, be privileged from arrest during their attendance at the session of their respective Houses, and in going to and returning from the same; and for any speech or debate in either House, they shall not be questioned in any other place.

No Senator or Representative shall, during the time for which he was elected, be appointed to any civil office under the authority of the United States, which shall have been created, or the emoluments whereof shall have been increased during such time: and no person holding any office under the United States, shall be a member of either House during his continuance in office.

The "Join, or Die" cartoon by Benjamin Franklin was first published in the Pennsylvania Gazette *and was used to encourage former colonies to unite against British rule.*

Section 7.—Revenue Bills, Legislative Process, Presidential Vet.

All bills for raising revenue shall originate in the House of Representatives; but the Senate may propose or concur with amendments as on other Bills.

Every bill which shall have passed the House of Representatives and the Senate, shall, before it become a law, be presented to the President of the United States; if he approve he shall sign it, but if not he shall return it, with his objections to that House in which it shall have originated, who shall enter the objections at large on their journal, and proceed to reconsider it. If after such reconsideration two thirds of that House shall agree to pass the bill, it shall be sent, together with the objections, to the other House, by which it shall likewise be reconsidered, and if approved by two thirds of that House, it shall become a law. But in all such cases the votes of both Houses shall be determined by yeas and nays, and the names of the persons voting for and against the bill shall be entered on the journal of each House respectively. If any bill shall not be returned by the President within ten days (Sundays excepted) after it shall have been presented to him, the same shall be a law, in like manner as if he had signed it, unless the Congress by their adjournment prevent its return, in which case it shall not be a law.

Every order, resolution, or vote to which the concurrence of the Senate and House of Representatives may be necessary (except on a question of adjournment) shall be presented to the President of the United States; and before the same shall take effect, shall be approved by him, or being disapproved by him, shall be repassed by two thirds of the Senate and House of Representatives, according to the rules and limitations prescribed in the case of a bill.

Section 8.—Powers of Congress

The Congress shall have power to lay and collect taxes, duties, imposts and excises, to pay the debts and provide for the common defense and general welfare of the United States; but all duties, imposts and excises shall be uniform throughout the United States;

To borrow money on the credit of the United States;

To regulate commerce with foreign nations, and among the several states, and with the Indian tribes;

To establish a uniform rule of naturalization, and uniform laws on the subject of bankruptcies throughout the United States;

To coin money, regulate the value thereof, and of foreign coin, and fix the standard of weights and measures;

To provide for the punishment of counterfeiting the securities and current coin of the United States;

To establish post offices and post roads;

To promote the progress of science and useful arts, by securing for limited times to authors and inventors the exclusive right to their respective writings and discoveries;

To constitute tribunals inferior to the Supreme Court;

To define and punish piracies and felonies committed on the high seas, and offenses against the law of nations;

To declare war, grant letters of marque and reprisal, and make rules concerning captures on land and water;

To raise and support armies, but no appropriation of money to that use shall be for a longer term than two years;

To provide and maintain a navy;

To make rules for the government and regulation of the land and naval forces;

To provide for calling forth the militia to execute the laws of the union, suppress insurrections and repel invasions;

Modern-day replica of a ship that would have been used in the original U.S. Navy

To provide for organizing, arming, and disciplining, the militia, and for governing such part of them as may be employed in the service of the United States, reserving to the states respectively, the appointment of the officers, and the authority of training the militia according to the discipline prescribed by Congress;

To exercise exclusive legislation in all cases whatsoever, over such District (not exceeding ten miles square) as may, by cession of particular states, and the acceptance of Congress, become the seat of the government of the United States, and to exercise like authority over all places purchased by the consent of the legislature of the state in which the same shall be, for the erection of forts, magazines, arsenals, dock-yards, and other needful buildings;—And

To make all laws which shall be necessary and proper for carrying into execution the foregoing powers, and all other powers vested by this Constitution in the government of the United States, or in any department or officer thereof.

Section 9.—Limits on Congress

The migration or importation of such persons as any of the states now existing shall think proper to admit, shall not be prohibited by the Congress prior to the year one thousand eight hundred and eight, but a tax or duty may be imposed on such importation, not exceeding ten dollars for each person.

The privilege of the writ of habeas corpus shall not be suspended, unless when in cases of rebellion or invasion the public safety may require it.

No bill of attainder or ex post facto Law shall be passed.

(This next part is clarified by the 16th Amendment)

No capitation, or other direct, tax shall be laid, unless in proportion to the census or enumeration herein before directed to be taken.

No tax or duty shall be laid on articles exported from any state.

No preference shall be given by any regulation of commerce or revenue to the ports of one state over those of another: nor shall vessels bound to, or from, one state, be obliged to enter, clear or pay duties in another.

No money shall be drawn from the treasury, but in consequence of appropriations made by law; and a regular statement and account of receipts and expenditures of all public money shall be published from time to time.

No title of nobility shall be granted by the United States: and no person holding any office of profit or trust under them, shall, without the consent of the Congress, accept of any present, emolument, office, or title, of any kind whatever, from any king, prince, or foreign state.

Section 10.—Powers Prohibited States

No state shall enter into any treaty, alliance, or confederation; grant letters of marque and reprisal; coin money; emit bills of credit; make anything but gold and silver coin a tender in payment

James Madision

of debts; pass any bill of attainder, ex post facto law, or law impairing the obligation of contracts, or grant any title of nobility.

No state shall, without the consent of the Congress, lay any imposts or duties on imports or exports, except what may be absolutely necessary for executing it's inspection laws: and the net produce of all duties and imposts, laid by any state on imports or exports, shall be for the use of the treasury of the United States; and all such laws shall be subject to the revision and control of the Congress.

No state shall, without the consent of Congress, lay any duty of tonnage, keep troops, or ships of war in time of peace, enter into any agreement or compact with another state, or with a foreign power, or engage in war, unless actually invaded, or in such imminent danger as will not admit of delay.

ARTICLE II—THE EXECUTIVE BRANCH

Section 1.—The President

The executive power shall be vested in a President of the United States of America. He shall hold his office during the term of four years, and, together with the Vice President, chosen for the same term, be elected, as follows:

Each state shall appoint, in such manner as the Legislature thereof may direct, a number of electors, equal to the whole number of Senators and Representatives to which the State may be entitled in the Congress: but no Senator or Representative, or person holding an office of trust or profit under the United States, shall be appointed an elector.

(The following clause superseded by the 12th Amendment)

The electors shall meet in their respective states, and vote by ballot for two persons, of whom one at least shall not be an inhabitant of the same state with themselves. And they shall make a list of all the persons voted for, and of the number of votes for each; which list they shall sign and certify, and transmit sealed to the seat of the government of the United States, directed to the President of the Senate. The President of the Senate shall, in the presence of the Senate and House of Representatives, open all the certificates, and the votes shall then be counted. The person having the greatest number of votes shall be the President, if such number be a majority of the whole number of electors appointed; and if there be more than one who have such majority, and have an equal number of votes, then the House of Representatives shall immediately choose by ballot one of them for President; and if no person have a majority, then from the five highest on the list the said House shall in like manner choose the President. But in choosing the President, the votes shall be taken by States, the representation from each state having one vote; A quorum for this purpose shall consist of a member or members from two thirds of the states, and a majority of all the states shall be necessary to a choice. In every case, after the choice of the President, the person having the greatest number of votes of the electors shall be the Vice President. But if there should remain two or more who have equal votes, the Senate shall choose from them by ballot the Vice President.

The Congress may determine the time of choosing the electors, and the day on which they shall give their votes; which day shall be the same throughout the United States.

No person except a natural born citizen, or a citizen of the United States, at the time of the adoption of this Constitution, shall be eligible to the office of President; neither shall any person be eligible to that office who shall not have attained to the age of

Nathaniel Currier's hand-colored lithograph entitled Presidents of the United States, 1844. *His piece depicts the ten first presidents.*

thirty five years, and been fourteen Years a resident within the United States.

(The following clause modified by the 20th and the 25th Amendments)

In case of the removal of the President from office, or of his death, resignation, or inability to discharge the powers and duties of the said office, the same shall devolve on the Vice President, and the Congress may by law provide for the case of removal, death, resignation or inability, both of the President and Vice President, declaring what officer shall then act as President, and such officer shall act accordingly, until the disability be removed, or a President shall be elected.

The President shall, at stated times, receive for his services, a compensation, which shall neither be increased nor diminished during the period for which he shall have been elected, and he shall not receive within that period any other emolument from the United States, or any of them.

Before he enter on the execution of his office, he shall take the following oath or affirmation: "I do solemnly swear (or affirm) that I will faithfully execute the office of President of the United States, and will to the best of my ability, preserve, protect and defend the Constitution of the United States."

Section 2.—Civilian Power over Military, Cabinet, Pardon Power, Appointments

The President shall be commander in chief of the Army and Navy of the United States, and of the militia of the several states, when called into the actual service of the United States; he may require the opinion, in writing, of the principal officer in each of the executive departments, upon any subject relating to the duties of their respective offices, and he shall have power to grant reprieves and pardons for offenses against the United States, except in cases of impeachment.

He shall have power, by and with the advice and consent of the Senate,

A vintage illustration of George Washington, the first President of the United States of America

to make treaties, provided two thirds of the Senators present concur; and he shall nominate, and by and with the advice and consent of the Senate, shall appoint ambassadors, other public ministers and consuls, judges of the Supreme Court, and all other officers of the United States, whose appointments are not herein otherwise provided for, and which shall be established by law: but the Congress may by law vest the appointment of such inferior officers, as they think proper, in the President alone, in the courts of law, or in the heads of departments.

The President shall have power to fill up all vacancies that may happen during the recess of the Senate, by granting commissions which shall expire at the end of their next session.

Section 3.—State of the Union, Convening Congress

He shall from time to time give to the Congress information of the state of the union, and recommend to their consideration such measures as he shall judge necessary and expedient; he may, on extraordinary occasions, convene both Houses, or either of them, and in case of disagreement between them, with respect to the time of adjournment, he may adjourn them to such time as he shall think proper; he shall receive ambassadors and other public ministers; he shall take care that the laws be faithfully executed, and shall commission all the officers of the United States.

Section 4.—Disqualification

The President, Vice President and all civil officers of the United States, shall be removed from office on impeachment for, and conviction of, treason, bribery, or other high crimes and misdemeanors.

ARTICLE III—THE JUDICIAL BRANCH

Section 1.—Judicial Powers

The judicial power of the United States, shall be vested in one Supreme Court, and in such inferior courts as the Congress may from time to time ordain and establish. The judges, both of the supreme and inferior courts, shall hold their offices during good behaviour, and shall, at stated times, receive for their services, a compensation, which shall not be diminished during their continuance in office.

Section 2.—Trial by Jury, Original Jurisdiction, Jury Trials

(The following modified by the 11th Amendment)

The judicial power shall extend to all cases, in law and equity, arising under this Constitution, the laws of the United States, and

This painting by Howard Chandler Christy depicts the signing of the Constitution

treaties made, or which shall be made, under their authority;—to all cases affecting ambassadors, other public ministers and consuls;—to all cases of admiralty and maritime jurisdiction;—to controversies to which the United States shall be a party;—to controversies between two or more states;—between a state and citizens of another state;—between citizens of different states;—between citizens of the same state claiming lands under grants of different states, and between a state, or the citizens thereof, and foreign states, citizens or subjects.

In all cases affecting ambassadors, other public ministers and consuls, and those in which a state shall be party, the Supreme Court shall have original jurisdiction. In all the other cases before mentioned, the Supreme Court shall have appellate jurisdiction, both as to law and fact, with such exceptions, and under such regulations as the Congress shall make.

The trial of all crimes, except in cases of impeachment, shall be by jury; and such trial shall be held in the state where the said crimes shall have been committed; but when not committed within any state, the trial shall be at such place or places as the Congress may by law have directed.

Section 3.—Treason

Treason against the United States, shall consist only in levying war against them, or in adhering to their enemies, giving them aid and comfort. No person shall be convicted of treason unless on the testimony of two witnesses to the same overt act, or on confession in open court.

The Congress shall have power to declare the punishment of treason, but no attainder of treason shall work corruption of blood, or forfeiture except during the life of the person attainted.

ARTICLE IV—THE STATES

Section 1.—Each State to Honor All Others

Full faith and credit shall be given in each state to the public acts, records, and judicial proceedings of every other state. And the Congress may by general laws prescribe the manner in which such acts, records, and proceedings shall be proved, and the effect thereof.

Section 2.—State Citizens, Extradition

The citizens of each state shall be entitled to all privileges and immunities of citizens in the several states.

A person charged in any state with treason, felony, or other crime, who shall flee from justice, and be found in another state, shall on demand of the executive authority of the state from which he fled, be delivered up, to be removed to the state having jurisdiction of the crime.

(The following clause is superseded by the 13th Amendment)

No person held to service or labor in one state, under the laws thereof, escaping into another, shall, in consequence of any law or regulation therein, be discharged from such service or labor, but shall be delivered up on claim of the party to whom such service or labor may be due.

Section 3.—New States

New states may be admitted by the Congress into this union; but no new states shall be formed or erected within the jurisdiction of any other state; nor any state be formed by the junction of two or more states, or parts of states, without the consent of the legislatures of the states concerned as well as of the Congress.

The Congress shall have power to dispose of and make all needful rules and regulations respecting the territory or other property belonging to the United States; and nothing in this

Constitution shall be so construed as to prejudice any claims of the United States, or of any particular state.

Section 4.—Republican Government

The United States shall guarantee to every state in this union a republican form of government, and shall protect each of them against invasion; and on application of the legislature, or of the executive (when the legislature cannot be convened) against domestic violence.

ARTICLE V—AMENDMENT PROCESS

The Congress, whenever two thirds of both houses shall deem it necessary, shall propose amendments to this Constitution, or, on the application of the legislatures of two thirds of the several states, shall call a convention for proposing amendments, which, in either case, shall be valid to all intents and purposes, as part of this Constitution, when ratified by the legislatures of three fourths of the several states, or by conventions in three fourths thereof, as the one or the other mode of ratification may be proposed by the Congress; provided that no amendment which may be made prior to the year one thousand eight hundred and eight shall in any manner affect the first and fourth clauses in the ninth section of the first article; and that no state, without its consent, shall be deprived of its equal suffrage in the Senate.

ARTICLE VI—SUPREMACY OF THE CONSTITUTION

All debts contracted and engagements entered into, before the adoption of this Constitution, shall be as valid against the United States under this Constitution, as under the Confederation.

This Constitution, and the laws of the United States which shall be made in pursuance thereof; and all treaties made, or which shall be made, under the authority of the United States, shall be the supreme law of the land; and the judges in every state shall be bound thereby, anything in the Constitution or laws of any State to the contrary notwithstanding.

The Senators and Representatives before mentioned, and the members of the several state legislatures, and all executive and judicial officers, both of the United States and of the several states, shall be bound by oath or affirmation, to support this Constitution; but no religious test shall ever be required as a qualification to any office or public trust under the United States.

The current Supreme Court House in Washington, D.C.

ARTICLE VII—RATIFICATION

The ratification of the conventions of nine states, shall be sufficient for the establishment of this Constitution between the states so ratifying the same.

SIGNATORIES

Done in convention by the unanimous consent of the states present the seventeenth day of September in the year of our Lord one thousand seven hundred and eighty seven and of the independence of the United States of America the twelfth.

In witness whereof We have hereunto subscribed our Names,

G. Washington Presidt and deputy from Virginia

Delaware: Geo. Read, Gunning Bedford, jun., John Dickinson, Richard Bassett, Jacob Broom

Maryland: James McHenry, Dan of St Thos. Jenifer, Danl. Carroll

Virginia: John Blair, James Madison Jr.

North Carolina: Wm. Blount, Richd. Dobbs Spaight, Hu Williamson

South Carolina: J. Rutledge, Charles Cotesworth Pinckney, Charles Pinckney, Pierce Butler

Georgia: William Few, Abr Baldwin

New Hampshire: John Langdon, Nicholas Gilman

Massachusetts: Nathaniel Gorham, Rufus King

Connecticut: Wm. Saml. Johnson, Roger Sherman

New York: Alexander Hamilton

New Jersey: Wil. Livingston, David Brearley, Wm. Paterson, Jona. Dayton

Pennsylvania: B Franklin, Thomas Mifflin, Robt. Morris, Geo. Clymer, Thos. FitzSimons, Jared Ingersoll, James Wilson, Gouv Morris

Honoring the Bill of Rights. Freedom checking tyranny, 1966.

THE BILL OF RIGHTS

★ ★ ★

In August of 1789, James Madison stood before the newly created, first ever United States House of Representatives and proposed a dozen Articles, or Amendments to the recently ratified Constitution. There was some debate, but by the 21st of the month, the House had accepted ten of the twelve Articles, and on September 25th of that year, by a joint resolution of the whole Congress these ten Amendments were proposed for ratification by the States. Two years later, on December 15th, 1791, having been ratified by three-fourths of the States, these ten Amendments became the law of the land. They were known then as they are today as the Bill of Rights.

If the original Constitution—the first seven articles–was all about establishing Union and organizing and empowering a National Government, this Bill of Rights–the first ten Amendments–was all about setting limits to that power, and protecting the individual from sanction from the Government for exercising these rights. We should remember, this protection is not complete. For example, the Government may not punish or otherwise sanction you for saying whatever's on your mind, but you may very well be sanctioned by your employer, or party, or even another individual for speaking up.

THE BILL OF RIGHTS

AMENDMENT I

Freedom of Religion, Speech, Press, Assembly, Petition—1791

Congress shall make no law respecting an establishment of religion, or prohibiting the free exercise thereof; or abridging the freedom of speech, or of the press; or the right of the people peaceably to assemble, and to petition the government for a redress of grievances.

AMENDMENT II

Right to Bear Arms—1791

A well regulated militia, being necessary to the security of a free state, the right of the people to keep and bear arms, shall not be infringed.

AMENDMENT III

Quartering of Troops—1791

No soldier shall, in time of peace be quartered in any house, without the consent of the owner, nor in time of war, but in a manner to be prescribed by law.

Before the Revolution, Fraunce's Tavern in New York was a meeting place for the Sons of Liberty.

AMENDMENT IV

Search and Seizure—1791

The right of the people to be secure in their persons, houses, papers, and effects, against unreasonable searches and seizures, shall not be violated, and no warrants shall issue, but upon probable cause, supported by oath or affirmation, and particularly describing the place to be searched, and the persons or things to be seized.

Federal Hall at the intersection of Wall and Broad Street, 1797

AMENDMENT V

Grand Jury, Double Jeopardy, Self-Incrimination, Due Process—1791

No person shall be held to answer for a capital, or otherwise infamous crime, unless on a presentment or indictment of a grand jury, except in cases arising in the land or naval forces, or in the militia, when in actual service in time of war or public danger; nor shall any person be subject for the same offense to be twice put in jeopardy of life or limb; nor shall be compelled in any criminal case to be a witness against himself, nor be deprived of life, liberty, or property, without due process of law; nor shall private property be taken for public use, without just compensation.

AMENDMENT VI

Criminal Prosecutions—Jury Trial, Right to Confront and to Counsel—1791

Patrick Henry

In all criminal prosecutions, the accused shall enjoy the right to a speedy and public trial, by an impartial jury of the state and district wherein the crime shall have been committed, which district shall have been previously ascertained by law, and to be informed of the nature and cause of the accusation; to be confronted with the witnesses against him; to have compulsory process for obtaining witnesses in his favor, and to have the assistance of counsel for his defense.

AMENDMENT VII

Common Law Suits—Jury Trial—1791

In suits at common law, where the value in controversy shall exceed twenty dollars, the right of trial by jury shall be preserved, and no fact tried by a jury, shall be otherwise reexamined in any court of the United States, than according to the rules of the common law.

AMENDMENT VIII

Excess Bail or Fines, Cruel and Unusual Punishment—1791

Excessive bail shall not be required, nor excessive fines imposed, nor cruel and unusual punishments inflicted.

AMENDMENT IX

Non-enumerated Rights—1791

The enumeration in the Constitution, of certain rights, shall not be construed to deny or disparage others retained by the people.

AMENDMENT X

Rights Reserved to States—1791

The powers not delegated to the United States by the Constitution, nor prohibited by it to the states, are reserved to the states respectively, or to the people.

Chamber of the first House of Representatives, Federal Hall, New York, 1789

FURTHER AMENDMENTS TO THE U.S. CONSTITUTION

★ ★ ★

Thanks to Article V, we're able, at need, to change, add to—amend in short—the Constitution. Thus we call it a "living document." It is almost as though the Founders rose from their work, dusted of their hands, slapped each other on the back, turned to their posterity and said "Oh, by the way—there's more to follow." They recognized that the exigencies and imperatives of their own time might not be wholly sufficient for future Americans. They expected this would be the case, and this insight has been key to the continued success of our Republic, and to the further perfection of our Union.

It is not easy to amend the Constitution. This is as it should be. We don't want to go changing our founding document every time the popular wind shifts. This very difficulty ensures that we don't change the supreme law of the land without a clear and popular consensus of the people. For the most part this has worked well.

AMENDMENT XI—SUITS AGAINST A STATE—1795

The judicial power of the United States shall not be construed to extend to any suit in law or equity, commenced or prosecuted against one of the United States by citizens of another state, or by citizens or subjects of any foreign state.

AMENDMENT XII—ELECTION OF PRESIDENT AND VICE-PRESIDENT—1804

The electors shall meet in their respective states and vote by ballot for President and Vice-President, one of whom, at least, shall not be an inhabitant of the same state with themselves; they shall name in their ballots the person voted for as President, and in distinct ballots the person voted for as Vice-President, and they shall make distinct lists of all persons voted for as President, and of all persons voted for as Vice-President, and of the number of votes for each, which lists they shall sign and certify, and transmit sealed to the seat of the government of the United States, directed to the President of the Senate;—The President of the Senate shall, in the presence of the Senate and House of Representatives, open all the certificates and the votes shall then be counted;—the person having the greatest number of votes for President, shall be the President, if such number be a majority of the whole number of electors appointed; and if no person have such majority, then from the persons having the highest numbers not exceeding three on the list of those voted for as President, the House of Representatives shall choose immediately, by ballot, the President. But in choosing the President, the votes shall be taken by states, the representation from each state having one vote; a quorum for this purpose shall consist of a member or members from two-thirds of the states, and a majority of all the states shall be necessary to a choice. And if the House of Representatives shall not choose a President whenever the right of choice shall devolve upon them, before the fourth day of March next following, then the Vice-President shall act as President, as in the case of the death or other constitutional disability of the President. The person having the greatest number of votes as Vice-President, shall be the Vice-President, if such number be a majority of the whole number of electors appointed, and if no person have a majority, then from the two highest numbers on the list, the Senate shall choose the Vice-President; a quorum for the purpose shall consist of two-thirds of the whole number of Senators, and a majority of the whole number shall be necessary to a choice. But no person constitutionally ineligible to the office of President shall be eligible to that of Vice-President of the United States.

AMENDMENT XIII—ABOLITION OF SLAVERY—1865

Section 1.

Neither slavery nor involuntary servitude, except as a punishment for crime whereof the party shall have been duly convicted, shall exist within the United States, or any place subject to their jurisdiction.

Section 2.

Congress shall have power to enforce this article by appropriate legislation.

AMENDMENT XIV—PRIVILEGES AND IMMUNITIES, DUE PROCESS, EQUAL PROTECTION, APPORTIONMENT OF REPRESENTATIVES, CIVIL WAR DISQUALIFICATION AND DEBT—1868

Section 1.

All persons born or naturalized in the United States, and subject to the jurisdiction thereof, are citizens of the United States and of the state wherein they reside. No state shall make or enforce any law which shall abridge the privileges or immunities of citizens of the United States; nor shall any state deprive any person of life, liberty, or property, without due process of law; nor deny to any person within its jurisdiction the equal protection of the laws.

Section 2.

Representatives shall be apportioned among the several states according to their respective numbers, counting the whole number of persons in each state, excluding Indians not taxed. But when the right to vote at any election for the choice of electors for President and Vice President of the United States, Representatives in Congress, the executive and judicial officers of a state, or the members of the legislature thereof, is denied to any of the male inhabitants of such state,

Lincoln Memorial

being twenty-one years of age, and citizens of the United States, or in any way abridged, except for participation in rebellion, or other crime, the basis of representation therein shall be reduced in the proportion which the number of such male citizens shall bear to the whole number of male citizens twenty-one years of age in such state.

Section 3.

No person shall be a Senator or Representative in Congress, or elector of President and Vice President, or hold any office, civil or military, under the United States, or under any state, who, having previously taken an oath, as a member of Congress, or as an officer of the United States, or as a member of any state legislature, or as an executive or judicial officer of any state, to support the Constitution of the United States, shall have engaged in insurrection or rebellion against the same, or given aid or comfort to the enemies thereof. But Congress may by a vote of two-thirds of each House, remove such disability.

Section 4.

The validity of the public debt of the United States, authorized by law, including debts incurred for payment of pensions and bounties for services in suppressing insurrection or rebellion, shall not be questioned. But neither the United States nor any state shall assume or pay any debt or obligation incurred in aid of insurrection or rebellion against the United States, or any claim for the loss or emancipation of any slave; but all such debts, obligations and claims shall be held illegal and void.

Section 5.

The Congress shall have power to enforce, by appropriate legislation, the provisions of this article.

AMENDMENT XV—RIGHTS NOT TO BE DENIED ON ACCOUNT OF RACE—1870

Section 1.

The right of citizens of the United States to vote shall not be denied or abridged by the United States or by any state on account of race, color, or previous condition of servitude.

Section 2.

The Congress shall have power to enforce this article by appropriate legislation.

AMENDMENT XVI—INCOME TAX—1913

The Congress shall have power to lay and collect taxes on incomes, from whatever source derived, without apportionment among the several states, and without regard to any census or enumeration.

AMENDMENT XVII—ELECTION OF SENATORS—1913

The Senate of the United States shall be composed of two Senators from each state, elected by the people thereof, for six years; and each Senator shall have one vote. The electors in each state shall have the qualifications requisite for electors of the most numerous branch of the state legislatures.

When vacancies happen in the representation of any state in the Senate, the executive authority of such state shall issue writs of election to fill such vacancies: Provided, that the legislature of any state may empower the executive thereof to make temporary

The ship America of Charleston *upon the Grand Banks 1789*

appointments until the people fill the vacancies by election as the legislature may direct.

This amendment shall not be so construed as to affect the election or term of any Senator chosen before it becomes valid as part of the Constitution.

AMENDMENT XVIII—PROHIBITION—1919

Section 1.

After one year from the ratification of this article the manufacture, sale, or transportation of intoxicating liquors within, the importation thereof into, or the exportation thereof from the United States and all territory subject to the jurisdiction thereof for beverage purposes is hereby prohibited.

Section 2.

The Congress and the several states shall have concurrent power to enforce this article by appropriate legislation.

Section 3.

This article shall be inoperative unless it shall have been ratified as an amendment to the Constitution by the legislatures of the several states, as provided in the Constitution, within seven years from the date of the submission hereof to the states by the Congress.

AMENDMENT XIX—WOMEN'S RIGHT TO VOTE—1920

The right of citizens of the United States to vote shall not be denied or abridged by the United States or by any state on account of sex.

Congress shall have power to enforce this article by appropriate legislation.

Vintage stamp of suffragettes and women voters from the 1970s

AMENDMENT XX—PRESIDENTIAL TERM AND SUCCESSION—1933

Section 1.

The terms of the President and Vice President shall end at noon on the 20th day of January, and the terms of Senators and Representatives at noon on the 3d day of January, of the years in which such terms would have ended if this article had not been ratified; and the terms of their successors shall then begin.

Section 2.

The Congress shall assemble at least once in every year, and such meeting shall begin at noon on the 3d day of January, unless they shall by law appoint a different day.

Section 3.

If, at the time fixed for the beginning of the term of the President, the President elect shall have died, the Vice President elect shall become President. If a President shall not have been chosen before the time fixed for the beginning of his term, or if the President elect shall have failed to qualify, then the Vice President elect shall act as President until a President shall have qualified; and the Congress may by law provide for the case wherein neither a President elect nor a Vice President elect shall have qualified, declaring who shall then act as President, or the manner in which one who is to act shall be selected, and such person shall act accordingly until a President or Vice President shall have qualified.

Section 4.

The Congress may by law provide for the case of the death of any of the persons from whom the House of Representatives may choose a President whenever the right of choice shall have devolved upon them, and for the case of the death of any of the persons from whom the Senate may choose a Vice President whenever the right of choice shall have devolved upon them.

Section 5.

Sections 1 and 2 shall take effect on the 15th day of October following the ratification of this article.

Section 6.

This article shall be inoperative unless it shall have been ratified as an amendment to the Constitution by the legislatures of three-fourths of the several states within seven years from the date of its submission.

AMENDMENT XXI—REPEAL OF PROHIBITION—1933

Removal of liquor during prohibition

Section 1.

The eighteenth article of amendment to the Constitution of the United States is hereby repealed.

Section 2.

The transportation or importation into any state, territory, or possession of the United States for delivery or use therein of intoxicating liquors, in violation of the laws thereof, is hereby prohibited.

Section 3.

This article shall be inoperative unless it shall have been ratified as an amendment to the Constitution by conventions in the several states, as provided in the Constitution, within seven years from the date of the submission hereof to the states by the Congress.

AMENDMENT XXII—TWO TERM LIMIT ON PRESIDENT—1951

Section 1.

No person shall be elected to the office of the President more than twice, and no person who has held the office of President, or acted as President, for more than two years of a term to which some other person was elected President shall be elected to the office of the President more than once. But this article shall not apply to any person holding the office of President when this article was proposed by the Congress, and shall not prevent any person who may be holding the office of President, or acting as President, during the term within which this article becomes operative from holding the office of President or acting as President during the remainder of such term.

Section 2.

This article shall be inoperative unless it shall have been ratified as an amendment to the Constitution by the legislatures of

World war I poster by Howard Chandler Christy. The painting Patriotic League *includes an open blue triangle, the symbol of war relief work.*

three-fourths of the several states within seven years from the date of its submission to the states by the Congress.

AMENDMENT XXIII—PRESIDENTIAL VOTE IN D.C.—1961

Section 1.

The District constituting the seat of government of the United States shall appoint in such manner as the Congress may direct:

A number of electors of President and Vice President equal to the whole number of Senators and Representatives in Congress to which the District would be entitled if it were a state, but in no event more than the least populous state; they shall be in addition to those appointed by the states, but they shall be considered, for the purposes of the election of President and Vice President, to be electors appointed by a state; and they shall meet in the District and perform such duties as provided by the twelfth article of amendment.

Section 2.

The Congress shall have power to enforce this article by appropriate legislation.

AMENDMENT XXIV—POLL TAX—1964

Section 1.

The right of citizens of the United States to vote in any primary or other election for President or Vice President, for electors for President or Vice President, or for Senator or Representative in Congress, shall not be denied or abridged by the United States or any state by reason of failure to pay any poll tax or other tax.

Section 2.

The Congress shall have power to enforce this article by appropriate legislation.

AMENDMENT XXV—PRESIDENTIAL SUCCESSION—1967

Section 1.

In case of the removal of the President from office or of his death or resignation, the Vice President shall become President.

The White House today

Section 2.

Whenever there is a vacancy in the office of the Vice President, the President shall nominate a Vice President who shall take office upon confirmation by a majority vote of both Houses of Congress.

Section 3.

Whenever the President transmits to the President pro tempore of the Senate and the Speaker of the House of Representatives his written declaration that he is unable to discharge the powers and duties of his office, and until he transmits to them a written declaration to the contrary, such powers and duties shall be discharged by the Vice President as Acting President.

Section 4.

Whenever the Vice President and a majority of either the principal officers of the executive departments or of such other body as Congress may by law provide, transmit to the President pro tempore of the Senate and the Speaker of the House of Representatives their written declaration that the President is unable to discharge the powers and duties of his office, the Vice President shall immediately assume the powers and duties of the office as Acting President.

Thereafter, when the President transmits to the President pro tempore of the Senate and the Speaker of the House of Representatives his written declaration that no inability exists, he shall resume the powers and duties of his office unless the Vice President and a majority of either the principal officers of the executive department or of such other body as Congress may by law provide, transmit within four days to the President pro tempore of the Senate and the Speaker of the House of Representatives their written declaration that the President is unable to discharge the powers and duties of his office. Thereupon Congress shall decide the issue, assembling within forty-eight hours for that purpose if not in session. If the Congress, within twenty-one days after receipt of the latter written declaration, or, if Congress is not in session, within twenty-one days after Congress is required to assemble, determines by two-thirds vote of both Houses that the President is unable to discharge the powers and duties of his office, the Vice President shall continue to discharge the same as Acting President; otherwise, the President shall resume the powers and duties of his office.

AMENDMENT XXVI—RIGHT TO VOTE AT AGE 18—1971

Section 1.

The right of citizens of the United States, who are 18 years of age or older, to vote, shall not be denied or abridged by the United States or any state on account of age.

Section 2.

The Congress shall have the power to enforce this article by appropriate legislation.

AMENDMENT XXVII—COMPENSATION OF MEMBERS OF CONGRESS—1992

No law, varying the compensation for the services of the Senators and Representatives, shall take effect, until an election of Representatives shall have intervened.

APPENDIX

★ ★ ★

No one doubted Patrick Henry's love of liberty or his patriotism. He was after all the man who gave voice to the Revolution by famously crying "Give me Liberty or give me death!" But he did oppose ratification of the Constitution. He  profoundly mistrusted consolidation of power in a national government. He believed a free people were best served by a loose Confederation wherein the States were primary. Henry lost the argument and his state of Virginia eventually ratified the Constitution.

PATRICK HENRY'S ADDRESS TO THE VIRGINIA CONVENTION AGAINST RATIFICATION

Mr. Chairman, I wish I was possessed with talents, or possessed of any thing that might enable me to elucidate this great subject. I am not free from suspicion: I am apt to entertain doubts. I rose yesterday to ask a question which arose in my own mind. When I asked that question, I thought the meaning of my interrogation was obvious. The fate of this question and of America may depend on this. Have they said, We, the states? Have they made a proposal of a compact between states? If they had, this would be a confederation. It is otherwise most clearly a consolidated government. The question turns, sir, on that poor little thing—the expression, We, the *people*, instead of the *states*, of America. I need not take much pains to show that the principles of this system are extremely pernicious, impolitic, and dangerous. Is this a monarchy, like England—a compact between prince and people, with checks on the former to secure the liberty of the latter? Is this a confederacy, like Holland—an association of a number of independent states, each of which retains its individual sovereignty? It is not a democracy, wherein the people retain all their rights securely. Had these principles been adhered to, we should not have been brought to this alarming transition, from a confederacy to a consolidated government. We have no detail of these great considerations, which, in my opinion, ought to have abounded before we should recur to a government of this kind.

Here is a resolution as radical as that which separated us from Great Britain. It is radical in this transition; our rights and privileges are endangered, and the sovereignty of the states will be relinquished: and cannot we plainly see that this is actually the case? The rights of conscience, trial by jury, liberty of the press, all your immunities and franchises, all pretensions to human rights and privileges, are rendered insecure, if not lost, by this change, so loudly talked of by some, and inconsiderately by others. Is this tame relinquishment of rights worthy of freemen? Is it worthy of that manly fortitude that ought to characterize republicans? It is said eight states have adopted this plan. I declare that if twelve states and a half had adopted it, I would, with manly firmness, and in spite of an erring world, reject it. You are not to inquire how your trade may be increased, nor how you are to become a great and powerful people, but how your liberties can be secured; for liberty ought to be the direct end of your government.

Having premised these things, I shall, with the aid of my judgment and information, which, I confess, are not extensive, go into the discussion of this system more minutely. Is it necessary for your liberty that you should abandon those great rights by the adoption of this system? Is the relinquishment of the trial by jury and the liberty of the press necessary for your liberty? Will the abandonment of your most sacred rights tend to the security of your liberty? Liberty, the greatest of all

As a warning to Britain, Franklin's cartoon depicted the country stripped of her colonies, 1764.

earthly blessings—give us that precious jewel, and you may take every thing else! But I am fearful I have lived long enough to become an old-fashioned fellow. Perhaps an invincible attachment to the dearest rights of man may, in these refined, enlightened days, be deemed old-fashioned; if so, I am contented to be so. I say, the time has been when every pulse of my heart beat for American liberty, and which, I believe, had a counterpart in the breast of every true American; but suspicions have gone forth—suspicions of my integrity—publicly reported that my professions are not real. Twenty-three years ago was I supposed a traitor to my country? I was then said to be the bane of sedition, because I supported the rights of my country. I may be thought suspicious when I say our privileges and rights are in danger. But, sir, a number of the people of this country are weak enough to think these things are too true. I am happy to find that the gentleman on the other side declares they are groundless. But, sir, suspicion is a virtue as long as its object is the preservation of the public good, and as long as it stays within proper bounds: should it fall on me, I am contented: conscious rectitude is a powerful consolation. I trust there are many who think my professions for the public good to be real. Let your suspicion look to both sides. There are many on the other side, who possibly may have been persuaded to the necessity of these measures, which I conceive to be dangerous to your liberty. Guard with jealous attention the public liberty. Suspect every one who approaches that jewel. Unfortunately, nothing will preserve it but downright force. Whenever you give up that force, you are inevitably ruined. I am answered by gentlemen, that, though I might speak of terrors, yet the fact was, that we were surrounded by none of the dangers I apprehended. I conceive this new government to be one of those dangers: it has produced those horrors which distress many of our best citizens. We are come hither to preserve the poor commonwealth of Virginia, if it can be possibly done: something must be done to preserve your liberty and mine. The Confederation, this same despised government, merits, in my opinion, the highest encomium: it carried us through a long and dangerous war; it rendered us victorious in that bloody conflict with a powerful nation; it has secured us a territory greater than any European monarch possesses: and shall a government which has been thus strong and vigorous, be accused of imbecility, and abandoned for want of energy? Consider what you are about to do before you part with the government. Take longer time in reckoning things; revolutions like this have happened in almost every country in Europe; similar examples are to be found in ancient Greece and ancient Rome— instances of the people losing their liberty by their own carelessness and the ambition of a few. We are cautioned by the honorable gentleman, who presides, against faction and turbulence. I acknowledge that licentiousness is dangerous, and that it ought to be provided against: I acknowledge, also, the new form of government may effectually prevent it: yet there is another thing it will as effectually do—it will oppress and ruin the people.

There are sufficient guards placed against sedition and licentiousness; for, when power is given to this government to suppress these, or for any other purpose, the language it assumes is clear, express, and unequivocal; but when this Constitution speaks of privileges, there is an ambiguity, sir, a fatal ambiguity—an ambiguity which is very astonishing. In the clause under consideration, there is the strangest language that I can conceive. I mean, when it says that there shall not be more representatives than one for every thirty thousand. Now, sir, how easy is it to evade this privilege!

"The number shall not exceed one for every thirty thousand." This may be satisfied by one representative from each state. Let our numbers be ever so great, this immense continent may, by this artful expression, be reduced to have but thirteen representatives. I confess this construction is not natural; but the ambiguity of the expression lays a good ground for a quarrel. Why was it not clearly and unequivocally expressed, that they should be entitled to have one for every thirty thousand? This would have obviated all disputes; and was this difficult to be done? What is the inference? When population increases, and a state shall send representatives in this proportion, Congress may remand them, because the right of having one for every thirty thousand is not clearly expressed. This possibility of reducing the number to one for each state approximates to probability by that other expression—"but each state shall at least have one representative." Now, is it not clear that, from the first expression, the number might be reduced so much that some states should have no representatives at all, were it not for the insertion of this last expression? And as this is the only restriction upon them, we may fairly conclude that they may

I do acknowledge the UNITED STATES of AMERICA to be Free, Independent and Sovereign States, and declare that the people thereof owe no allegiance or obedience to George the Third, King of Great-Britain; and I renounce, refuse and abjure any allegiance or obedience to him; and I do that I will, to the utmost of my power, support, maintain and defend the said United States against the said King George the Third, his heirs and successors, and his or their abettors, assistants and adherents, and will serve the said United States in the office of which I now hold, with fidelity, according to the best of my skill and understanding.

Oath of Allegiance, 1776

restrain the number to one from each state. Perhaps the same horrors may hang over my mind again. I shall be told I am continually afraid: but, sir, I have strong cause of apprehension. In some parts of the plan before you, the great rights of freemen are endangered; in other parts, absolutely taken away. How does your trial by jury stand? In civil cases gone—not sufficiently secured in criminal—this best privilege is gone. But we are told that we need not fear; because those in power, being our representatives, will not abuse the powers we put in their hands. I am not well versed in history, but I will submit to your recollection, whether liberty has been destroyed most often by the licentiousness of the people, or by the tyranny of rulers. I imagine, sir, you will find the balance on the side of tyranny. Happy will you be if you miss the fate of those nations, who, omitting to resist their oppressors, or negligently suffering their liberty to be wrested from them, have groaned under intolerable despotism! Most of the human race are now in this deplorable condition; and those nations who have gone in search of grandeur, power, and splendor, have also fallen a sacrifice, and been the victims of their own folly. While they acquired those visionary blessings, they lost their freedom. My great objection to this government is, that it does not leave us the means of defending our rights, or of waging war against tyrants. It is urged by some gentlemen, that this new plan will bring us an acquisition of strength—an army, and the militia of the states. This is an idea extremely ridiculous: gentlemen cannot be earnest. This acquisition will trample on our fallen liberty. Let my beloved Americans guard against that fatal lethargy that has pervaded the universe. Have we the means of resisting disciplined armies, when our only defence, the militia, is put into the hands of Congress? The honorable gentleman said that great danger would ensue if the

Convention rose without adopting this system. I ask, Where is that danger? I see none. Other gentlemen have told us, within these walls, that the union is gone, or that the union will be gone. Is not this trifling with the judgment of their fellow-citizens? Till they tell us the grounds of their fears, I will consider them as imaginary. I rose to make inquiry where those dangers were; they could make no answer: I believe I never shall have that answer. Is there a disposition in the people of this country to revolt against the dominion of laws? Has there been a single tumult in Virginia? Have not the people of Virginia, when laboring under the severest pressure of accumulated distresses, manifested the most cordial acquiescence in the execution of the laws? What could be more awful than their unanimous acquiescence under general distresses? Is there any revolution in Virginia? Whither is the spirit of America gone? Whither is the genius of America fled? It was but yesterday, when our enemies marched in triumph through our country. Yet the people of this country could not be appalled by their pompous armaments: they stopped their career, and victoriously captured them. Where is the peril, now, compared to that? Some minds are agitated by foreign alarms. Happily for us, there is no real danger from Europe; that country is engaged in more arduous business: from that quarter there is no cause of fear: you may sleep in safety forever for them.

Where is the danger? If, sir, there was any, I would recur to the American spirit to defend us; that spirit which has enabled us to surmount the greatest difficulties: to that illustrious spirit I address my most fervent prayer to prevent our adopting a system destructive to liberty. Let not gentlemen be told that it is not safe to reject this government. Wherefore is it not safe? We are told there are dangers, but those dangers are ideal; they cannot be demonstrated.

To encourage us to adopt it, they tell us that there is a plain, easy way of getting amendments. When I come to contemplate this part, I suppose that I am mad, or that my countrymen are so. The way to amendment is, in my conception, shut. Let us consider this plain, easy way. "The Congress, whenever two thirds of both houses shall deem it necessary, shall propose amendments to this Constitution, or, on the application of the legislatures of two thirds of the several states, shall call a Convention for proposing amendments, which, in either case, shall be valid to all intents and purposes, as part of this Constitution, when ratified by the legislatures of three fourths of the several states, or by the Conventions in three fourths thereof, as the one or the other mode of ratification may be proposed by the Congress. Provided, that no amendment which may be made prior to the year 1808, shall in any manner affect the 1st and 4th clauses in the 9th section of the 1st article; and that no state, without its consent, shall be deprived of its equal suffrage in the Senate."

Hence it appears that three fourths of the states must ultimately agree to any amendments that may be necessary. Let us consider the consequence of this. However uncharitable it may appear, yet I must tell my opinion—that the most unworthy characters may get into power, and prevent the introduction of amendments. Let us suppose—for the case is suppos-

In Constantino Brumidi's painting Union, *he personifies the American flag as a young woman, 1869*

able, possible, and probable—that you happen to deal those powers to unworthy hands; will they relinquish powers already in their possession, or agree to amendments? Two thirds of the Congress, or of the state legislatures, are necessary even to propose amendments. If one third of these be unworthy men, they may prevent the application for amendments; but what is destructive and mischievous, is, that three fourths of the state legislatures, or of the state conventions, must concur in the amendments when proposed! In such numerous bodies, there must necessarily be some designing, bad men. To suppose that so large a number as three fourths of the states will concur, is to suppose that they will possess genius, intelligence, and integrity, approaching to miraculous. It would indeed be miraculous that they should concur in the same amendments, or even in such as would bear some likeness to one another; for four of the smallest states, that do not collectively contain one tenth part of the population of the United States, may obstruct the most salutary and necessary amendments. Nay, in these four states, six tenths of the people may reject these amendments; and suppose that amendments shall be opposed to amendments, which is highly probable,—is it possible that three fourths can ever agree to the same amendments? A bare majority in these four small states may hinder the adoption of amendments; so that we may fairly and justly conclude that one twentieth part of the American people may prevent the removal of the most grievous inconveniences and oppression, by refusing to accede to amendments. A trifling minority may reject the most salutary amendments. Is this an easy mode of securing the public liberty: It is, sir, a most fearful situation, when the most contemptible minority can prevent the alteration of the most oppressive government; for it may, in many respects, prove to be such. Is this the spirit of republicanism?

What, sir, is the genius of democracy? Let me read that clause of the bill of rights of Virginia which relates to this: 3d clause:— that government is, or ought to be, instituted for the common benefit, protection, and security of the people, nation, or community. Of all the various modes and forms of government, that is best, which is capable of producing the greatest degree of happiness and safety, and is most effectually secured against the danger of mal-administration; and that whenever any government shall be found inadequate, or contrary to those purposes, a majority of the community hath an indubitable, unalienable, and indefeasible right to reform, alter, or abolish it, in such manner as shall be judged most conducive to the public weal.

This, sir, is the language of democracy—that a majority of the community have a right to alter government when found to be oppressive. But how different is the genius of your new Constitution from this! How different from the sentiments of freemen, that a contemptible minority can prevent the good of the majority! If, then, gentlemen, standing on this ground, are come to that point, that they are willing to bind themselves and their posterity to be oppressed, I am amazed and inexpressibly astonished. If this be the opinion of the majority, I must submit; but to me, sir, it appears perilous and destructive. I cannot help thinking so. Perhaps it may be the result of my age. These may be feelings natural to a man of my years, when the American spirit has left him, and his mental powers, like the members of the body, are decayed. If, sir, amendments are left to the twentieth, or tenth part of the people of America, your liberty is gone forever. We have heard that there is a great deal of bribery practised in the House of Commons, in England, and that many of the members raise themselves to preferments by selling the rights of the whole of the people. But, sir, the tenth part of that body cannot continue oppression on the rest of the people. English liberty is, in this case, on a firmer foundation than American liberty. It will be easily contrived to procure the opposition of one tenth of the people to any alteration, however judicious. The honorable gentleman who presides told us that, to prevent abuses in our government, we will assemble in Convention, recall our delegated powers, and punish our servants for abusing the trust reposed in them. O sir, we should have fine times, indeed, if, to punish tyrants, it were only sufficient to assemble the people! Your arms, wherewith you could defend yourselves, are gone; and you have no longer an aristocratical, no longer a democratical spirit. Did you ever read of any revolution in a nation, brought about by the punishment of those in power, inflicted by those who had no power at all? You read of a riot act in a country which is called one of the freest in the world, where a few neighbors cannot assemble without the risk of being shot by a hired soldiery, the engines of despotism. We may see such an act in America.

A standing army we shall have, also, to execute the execrable commands of tyranny; and how are you to punish them? Will you order them to be punished? Who shall obey these orders? Will your mace-bearer be a match for a disciplined regiment? In what situation are we to be? The clause before you gives a power of direct taxation, unbounded and unlimited, exclusive power of legislation, in all cases whatsoever, for ten miles square, and over all places purchased for the erection of forts, magazines, arsenals, dockyards, &c. What resistance could be made? The attempt would be madness. You will find all the strength of this country in the hands of your enemies; their garrisons will naturally be the strongest places in the country. Your militia is given up to Congress, also, in another part of this plan: they will therefore act as they think proper: all power will be in their own possession. You cannot force them to receive their punishment: of what service would militia be to you, when, most probably, you will not have a single musket in the state? for, as arms are to be provided by Congress, they may or may not furnish them.

Let me here call your attention to that part which gives the Congress power "to provide for organizing, arming, and disciplining the militia, and for governing such part of them as may be employed in the service of the United States—reserving to the states, respectively, the appointment of the officers, and the authority of training the militia according to the discipline prescribed by Congress." By this, sir, you see that their control over our last and best defence is unlimited. If they neglect or refuse to discipline or arm our militia, they will be useless: the states can do neither—this power being exclusively given to Congress. The power of appointing officers over men not disciplined or armed is ridiculous; so that this pretended little remains of power left to the states may, at the pleasure of Congress, be rendered nugatory. Our situation will be deplorable indeed: nor can we ever expect to get this government amended, since I have already shown that a very small minority may prevent it, and that small minority interested in the continuance of the oppression. Will the oppressor let go the oppressed? Was there ever an instance? Can the annals of mankind exhibit one single example where rulers overcharged with power willingly let go the oppressed, though solicited and requested most earnestly? The application for amendments will therefore be fruitless. Sometimes, the oppressed have got loose by one of those bloody struggles that desolate a country; but a willing relinquishment of power is one of those things which human nature never was, nor ever will be, capable of.

The honorable gentleman's observations, respecting the people's right of being the agents in the formation of this government, are not accurate, in my humble conception. The distinction between a national government and a confederacy is not sufficiently discerned. Had the delegates, who were sent to Philadelphia, a power to propose a consolidated government instead of a confederacy? Were they not deputed by states, and not by the people? The assent of the people, in their collective capacity, is not necessary to the formation of a federal government. The people have no right to enter into leagues, alliances, or confederations; they are not the proper agents for this purpose. States and foreign powers are the only proper agents for this kind of government. Show me an instance where the people have exercised this business. Has it not always gone through the legislatures? I refer you to the treaties with France, Holland, and other nations. How were they made? Were they not made by the states? Are the people, therefore, in their aggregate capacity, the proper persons to form a confederacy? This, therefore, ought to depend on the consent of the legislatures, the people having never sent delegates to make any proposition for changing the government. Yet I must say, at the same time, that it was made on grounds the most pure;

and perhaps I might have been brought to consent to it so far as to the change

A birds eye view of New York City by John Bachmann, 1865

of government. But there is one thing in it which I never would acquiesce in. I mean, the changing it into a consolidated government, which is so abhorrent to my mind. [The honorable gentleman then went on to the figure we make with foreign nations; the contemptible one we make in France and Holland; which, according to the substance of the notes, he attributes to the present feeble government.] An opinion has gone forth, we find, that we are contemptible people: the time has been when we were thought otherwise. Under the same despised government, we commanded the respect of all Europe: wherefore are we now reckoned otherwise? The American spirit has fled from hence: it has gone to regions where it has never been expected; it has gone to the people of France, in search of a splendid government—a strong, energetic government. Shall we imitate the example of those nations who have gone from a simple to a splendid government? Are those nations more worthy of our imitation? What can make an adequate satisfaction to them for the loss they have suffered in attaining such a government—for the loss of their liberty? If we admit this consolidated government, it will be because we like a great, splendid one. Some way or other we must be a great and mighty empire; we must have an army, and a navy, and a number of things. When the American spirit was in its youth, the language of America was different: liberty, sir, was then the primary object. We are descended from a people whose government was founded on liberty: our glorious forefathers of Great Britain made liberty the foundation of every thing. That country is become a great, mighty, and splendid nation; not because their government is strong and energetic, but, sir, because liberty is its direct end and foundation. We drew the spirit of liberty from our British ancestors: by that spirit we have triumphed over every difficulty. But now, sir, the American spirit, assisted by

The doller coin depicts the American Bald Eagle, a symbol of the American Spirit

the ropes and chains of consolidation, is about to convert this country into a powerful and mighty empire. If you make the citizens of this country agree to become the subjects of one great consolidated empire of America, your government will not have sufficient energy to keep them together. Such a government is incompatible with the genius of republicanism. There will be no checks, no real balances, in this government. What can avail your specious, imaginary balances, your rope-dancing, chain-rattling, ridiculous ideal checks and contrivances? But, sir, we are not feared by foreigners; we do not make nations tremble. Would this constitute happiness, or secure liberty? I trust, sir, our political hemisphere will ever direct their operations to the security of those objects.

Consider our situation, sir: go to the poor man, and ask him what he does. He will inform you that he enjoys the fruits of his labor, under his own fig-tree, with his wife and children around him, in peace and security. Go to every other member of society,— you will find the same tranquil ease and content; you will find no alarms or disturbances. Why, then, tell us of danger, to terrify us into an adoption of this new form of government? And yet who knows the dangers that this new system may produce? They are out of the sight of the common people: they cannot foresee latent consequences. I dread the operation of it on the middling and lower classes of people: it is for them I fear the adoption of this system. I fear I tire the patience of the committee; but I beg to be indulged with a few more observations. When I thus profess myself an advocate for the liberty of the people, I shall be told I am a designing man, that I am to be a great man, that I am to be a demagogue; and many similar illiberal insinuations will be thrown out: but, sir, conscious rectitude outweighs those things with me. I see great jeopardy in this new government. I see none from our present one. I hope some gentleman or other will bring forth, in full array, those dangers, if there be any, that we may see and touch them. I have said that I thought this a consolidated government: I will now prove it. Will the great rights of the people be secured by this government? Suppose it should prove oppressive, how can it be altered? Our bill of rights declares, "that a majority of the community hath an indubitable, unalienable, and indefeasible right to reform, alter, or abolish it, in such manner as shall be judged most conducive to the public weal."

I have just proved that one tenth, or less, of the people of America—a most despicable minority—may prevent this reform or alteration. Suppose the people of Virginia should wish to alter their government; can a majority of them do it? No; because they are connected with other men, or, in other words, consolidated with other states. When the people of Virginia, at a future day, shall wish to alter their government, though they should be unanimous in this desire, yet they may be prevented therefrom by a despicable minority at the extremity of the United States. The founders of your own Constitution made your government changeable: but the power of changing it is gone from you. Whither is it gone? It is placed in the same hands that hold the rights of twelve other states;

and those who hold those rights have right and power to keep them. It is not the particular government of Virginia: one of the leading features of that government is, that a majority can alter it, when necessary for the public good. This government is not a Virginian, but an American government. Is it not, therefore, a consolidated government? The sixth clause of your bill of rights tells you, "that elections of members to serve as representatives of the people in Assembly ought to be free, and that all men having sufficient evidence of permanent common interest with, and attachment to, the community, have the right of suffrage, and cannot be *taxed*, or deprived of their property for public uses, without their own consent, or that of their representatives so elected, nor bound by any law to which they have not in like manner assented for the public good." But what does this Constitution say? The clause under consideration gives an unlimited and unbounded power of taxation. Suppose every delegate from Virginia opposes a law laying a tax; what will it avail? They are opposed by a majority; eleven members can destroy their efforts: those feeble ten cannot prevent the passing the most oppressive tax law; so that, in direct opposition to the spirit and express language of your declaration of rights, you are taxed, not by your own consent, but by people who have no connection with you.

The next clause of the bill of rights tells you, "that all power of suspending law, or the execution of laws, by any authority, without the consent of the representatives of the people, is injurious to their rights, and ought not to be exercised." This tells us that there can be no suspension of government or laws without our own consent; yet this Constitution can counteract and suspend any of our laws that contravene its oppressive operation; for they have the power of direct taxation, which suspends our bill of rights; and it is expressly provided that they can make all laws necessary for carrying their powers into execution; and it is declared paramount to the laws and constitutions of the states. Consider how the only remaining defence we have left is destroyed in this manner. Besides the expenses of maintaining the Senate and other house in as much splendor as they please, there is to be a great and mighty President, with very extensive powers—the powers of a king. He is to be supported in extravagant magnificence; so that the whole of our property may be taken by this American government, by laying what taxes they please, giving themselves what salaries they please, and suspending our laws at their pleasure. I might be thought too inquisitive, but I believe I should take up very little of your time in enumerating the little power that is left to the government of Virginia; for this power is reduced to little or nothing: their garrisons, magazines, arsenals, and forts, which will be situated in the strongest places within the states; their ten miles square, with all the fine ornaments of human life, added to their powers, and taken from the states, will reduce the power of the latter to nothing.

The voice of tradition, I trust, will inform posterity of our struggles for freedom. If our descendants be worthy the name of Americans, they will preserve, and hand down to their latest posterity, the transactions of the present times; and, though I confess my exclamations are not worthy the hearing, they will see that I have done my utmost to preserve their liberty; for I never will give up the power of direct taxation but for a scourge. I am willing to give it conditionally; that is, after non-compliance with requisitions. I will do more, sir, and what I hope will convince the most skeptical man that I am a lover of the American Union— that, in case Virginia shall not make punctual payment, the control of our custom-houses, and the whole regulation of trade, shall be given to Congress, and that Virginia shall depend on Congress even for passports, till Virginia shall have paid the last farthing, and furnished the last soldier. Nay, sir, there is another alternative to which I would consent;—even that they should strike us out of the Union, and take away from us all federal privileges, till we comply with federal requisitions: but let it depend upon our own pleasure to pay our money in the most easy manner for our people. Were all the states, more terrible than the mother country, to join against us, I hope Virginia could defend herself; but, sir, the disso-lution of the Union is most abhorrent to my mind. The first thing I have at heart is American liberty: the second thing is American union; and I hope the people of Virginia will endeavor to preserve that union. The increasing population of the Southern States is far greater than that of New England; consequently, in a short time,

The Gadsden flag is a historical American flag with a yellow field depicting a rattlesnake coiled and ready to strike. The flag was designed and named after American general Christopher Gadsden. The flag was used by the United States Marine Corps during the American Revolution.

they will be far more numerous than the people of that country. Consider this, and you will find this state more particularly interested to support American liberty, and not bind our posterity by an improvident relinquishment of our rights. I would give the best security for a punctual compliance with requisitions; but I beseech gentlemen, at all hazards, not to give up this unlimited power of taxation. The honorable gentleman has told us that these powers, given to Congress, are accompanied by a judiciary which will correct all. On examination, you will find this very judiciary oppressively constructed; your jury trial destroyed, and the judges dependent on Congress.

In this scheme of energetic government, the people will find two sets of tax-gatherers—the state and the federal sheriffs. This, it seems to me, will produce such dreadful oppression as the people cannot possibly bear. The federal sheriff may commit what oppression, make what distresses, he pleases, and ruin you with impunity; for how are you to tie his hands? Have you any sufficiently decided means of preventing him from sucking your blood by speculations, commissions, and fees? Thus thousands of your people will be most shamefully robbed: our state sheriffs, those unfeeling blood-suckers have, under the watchful eye of our legislature, committed the most horrid and barbarous ravages on our people. It has required the most constant vigilance of the legislature to keep them from totally ruining the people; a repeated succession of laws has been made to suppress their iniquitous speculations and cruel extortions; and as often has their nefarious ingenuity devised methods of evading the force of those laws: in the struggle they have generally triumphed over the legislature.

It is a fact that lands have been sold for five shillings, which were worth one hundred pounds: if sheriffs, thus immediately under the eye of our state legislature and judiciary, have dared to commit these outrages, what would they not have done if their masters had been at Philadelphia or New York? If they perpetrate the most unwarrantable outrage on your person or property, you cannot get redress on this side of Philadelphia or New York; and how can you get it there? If your domestic avocations could permit you to go thither, there you must appeal to judges sworn to support this Constitution, in opposition to that of any state, and who may also be inclined to favor their own officers. When these harpies are aided by excisemen, who may search, at any time, your houses, and most secret recesses, will the people bear it? If you think so, you differ from me. Where I thought there was a possibility of such mischiefs, I would grant power with a niggardly hand; and here there is a strong probability that these oppressions shall actu-

The Senate's side of the capital building in Washington, D.C.

ally happen. I may be told that it is safe to err on that side, because such regulations may be made by Congress as shall restrain these officers, and because laws are made by our representatives, and judged by righteous judges: but, sir, as these regulations may be made, so they may not; and many reasons there are to induce a belief that they will not. I shall therefore be an infidel on that point till the day of my death.

This Constitution is said to have beautiful features; but when I come to examine these features, sir, they appear to me horribly frightful. Among other deformities, it has an awful squinting; it squints towards monarchy; and does not this raise indignation in the breast of every true American?

Your President may easily become king. Your Senate is so imperfectly constructed that your dearest rights may be sacrificed by what may be a small minority; and a very small minority may continue forever unchangeably this government, although horridly defective. Where are your checks in this government? Your strongholds will be in the hands of your enemies. It is on a supposition that your American governors shall be honest, that all the good qualities of this government are founded; but its defective and imperfect construction puts it in their power to perpetrate the worst of mischiefs, should they be bad men; and, sir, would not all the world, from the eastern to the western hemisphere, blame our distracted folly in resting our rights upon the contingency of our rulers being good or bad? Show me that age and country where the rights and liberties of the people were placed on the sole chance of their rulers being good men, without a consequent loss of liberty! I say that the loss of that dearest privilege has ever followed, with absolute certainty, every such mad attempt.

If your American chief be a man of ambition and abilities, how easy is it for him to render himself absolute! The army is in his hands, and if he be a man of address, it will be attached to him, and it will be the subject of long meditation with him to seize the first auspicious moment to accomplish his design; and, sir, will the American spirit solely relieve you when this happens? I would rather infinitely—and I am sure most of this Convention are of the same opinion—have a king, lords, and commons, than a government so replete with such insupportable evils. If we make a king, we may prescribe the rules by which he shall rule his people, and interpose such checks as shall prevent him from infringing them; but the President, in the field, at the head of his army, can prescribe the terms on which he shall reign master, so far that it will puzzle any American ever to get his neck from under the galling yoke. I cannot with patience think of this idea. If ever he violates the laws, one of two things will happen: he will come at the head of his army, to carry every thing before him; or he will give bail, or do what Mr. Chief Justice will order him. If he be guilty, will not the recollection of his crimes teach him to make one bold push for the American throne? Will not the immense difference between being master of every thing, and being ignominiously tried and punished, powerfully excite him to make this bold push? But, sir, where is the existing force to punish him? Can he not, at the head of his army, beat down every opposition? Away with your President! we shall have a king: the army will salute him monarch: your militia will leave you, and assist in making him king, and fight against you: and what have you to oppose this force? What will then become of you and your rights? Will not absolute despotism ensue?

[Here Mr. HENRY strongly and pathetically expatiated on the probability of the President's enslaving America, and the horrid consequences that must result.]

What can be more defective than the clause concerning the elections? The control given to Congress over the time, place, and manner of holding elections, will totally destroy the end of suffrage. The elections may be held at one place, and the most inconvenient in the state; or they may be at remote distances from those who have a right of suffrage: hence nine out of ten must either not vote at all, or vote for strangers; for the most influential characters will be applied to, to know who are the most proper to be chosen. I repeat, that the control of Congress over the *manner*, &c., of electing, well warrants this idea. The natural consequence will be, that this democratic branch will possess none of the public

Salem, Massachusetts—a member of one of the original 13 colonies

confidence; the people will be prejudiced against representatives chosen in such an injudicious manner. The proceedings in the northern conclave will be hidden from the yeomanry of this country. We are told that the yeas and nays shall be taken, and entered on the journals. This, sir, will avail nothing: it may be locked up in their chests, and concealed forever from the people; for they are not to publish what parts they think require secrecy: they *may* think, and *will think*, the whole requires it. Another beautiful feature of this Constitution is, the publication from time to time of the receipts and expenditures of the public money.

This expression, *from time to time*, is very indefinite and indeterminate: it may extend to a century. Grant that any of them are wicked; they may squander the public money so as to ruin you, and yet this expression will give you no redress. I say they may ruin you; for where, sir, is the responsibility? The yeas and nays will show you nothing, unless they be fools as well as knaves; for, after having wickedly trampled on the rights of the people, they would act like fools indeed, were they to publish and divulge their iniquity, when they have it equally in their power to suppress and conceal it. Where is the responsibility—that leading principle in the British government? In that government, a punishment certain and inevitable is provided; but in this, there is no real, actual punishment for the grossest mal-administration. They may go without punishment, though they commit the most outrageous violation on our immunities. That paper may tell me they will be punished. I ask, By what law? They must make the law, for there is no existing law to do it. What! will they make a law to punish themselves?

This, sir, is my great objection to the Constitution, that there is no true responsibility—and that the preservation of our liberty depends on the single chance of men being virtuous enough to make laws to punish themselves.

In the country from which we are descended, they have real and not imaginary responsibility; for their mal-administration has cost their heads to some of the most saucy geniuses that ever were. The Senate, by making treaties, may destroy your liberty and laws for want of responsibility. Two thirds of those that shall happen to be present, can, with the President, make treaties that shall be the supreme law of the land; they may make the most ruinous treaties; and yet there is no punishment for them. Whoever shows me a punishment provided for them will oblige me. So, sir, notwithstanding there are eight pillars, they want another. Where will they make another? I trust, sir, the exclusion of the evils wherewith this system is replete in its present form, will be made a condition precedent to its adoption by this or any other state. The transition, from a general unqualified admission to offices, to a consolidation of government, seems easy; for, though the American states are dissimilar in their structure, this will assimilate them. This, sir, is itself a strong consolidating feature, and is not one of the least dangerous in that system. Nine states are sufficient to establish this government over those nine. Imagine that nine have come into it. Virginia has certain scruples. Suppose she will, consequently, refuse to join with those states; may not she still continue in friendship and union with them? If she sends her annual requisitions in dollars, do you think their stomachs will be so squeamish as to refuse her dollars? Will they not accept her regiments? They would intimidate you into an inconsiderate adoption, and frighten you with ideal evils, and that the Union shall be dissolved. 'Tis a bugbear, sir: the fact is, sir, that the eight adopting states can hardly stand on their own legs. Public fame tells us that the adopting states have already heart-burnings and animosity, and repent their precipitate hurry: this, sir, may occasion exceeding great mischief. When I reflect on these and many other circumstances, I must think those states will be found to be in confederacy with us. If we pay our quota of money annually, and furnish our ratable number of men, when necessary, I can see no danger from a rejection.

The history of Switzerland clearly proves that we might be in amicable alliance with those states without adopting this Constitution. Switzerland is a confederacy, consisting of dissimilar governments. This is an example which proves that governments of dissimilar structures may be confederated. That confederate republic has stood upwards of four hundred years; and, although several of the individual republics are democratic, and the rest aristocratic, no evil has resulted from this dissimilarity; for they have braved all the power of France and Germany during that long period. The Swiss spirit, sir, has kept them together; they have encountered and overcome immense difficulties with patience and fortitude. In the vicinity of powerful and ambitious monarchs, they have retained their independence, republican simplicity, and valor. [Here he makes a comparison of the people of that country and those of France, and makes a quotation from Addison illustrating the subject.] Look at the peasants of that country and of France; and mark the difference. You will find the condition of the former far more desirable and comfortable. No matter whether the people be great, splendid, and powerful, if they enjoy freedom. The Turkish Grand Signior, alongside of our President, would put us to disgrace; but we should be as abundantly consoled for this disgrace, when our citizens have been put in contrast with the Turkish slave. The most valuable end of government is the liberty of the inhabitants. No possible advantages can compensate for the loss of this privilege. Show me the reason why the American Union is to be dissolved. Who are those eight adopting states? Are they averse to give us a little time to consider, before we conclude? Would such a disposition render a junction with them eligible; or is it the genius of that kind of government to precipitate people hastily into measures of the utmost importance, and grant no indulgence? If it be, sir, is it for us to accede to such a government? We have a right to have time to consider; we shall therefore insist upon it. Unless the government be amended, we can never accept it. The adopting states will doubtless accept our money and our regiments; and what is to be the consequence, if we are disunited? I believe it is yet doubtful, whether it is not proper to stand by a while, and see the effect of its adoption in other states. In forming a government, the utmost care should be taken to prevent its becoming oppressive; and this government is of such an intricate

A flag flies over the Brooklyn bridge in New York City. John Roebling, the bridge's designer, famously said of his creation, "The bridge may sag, but it will not fall." Much like the American ideals set down by our forefathers.

and complicated nature, that no man on this earth can know its real operation. The other states have no reason to think, from the antecedent conduct of Virginia, that she has any intention of seceding from the Union, or of being less active to support the general welfare. Would they not, therefore, acquiesce in our taking time to deliberate—deliberate whether the measure be not perilous, not only for us, but the adopting states?

Permit me, sir, to say, that a great majority of the people, even in the adopting states, are averse to this government. I believe I would be right to say, that they have been egregiously misled. Pennsylvania has, *perhaps*, been tricked into it. If the other states who have adopted it have not been tricked, still they were too much hurried into its adoption. There were very respectable minorities in several of them; and if reports be true, a clear majority of the people are averse to it. If we also accede, and it should prove grievous, the peace and prosperity of our country, which we all love, will be destroyed. This government has not the affection of the people at present. Should it be oppressive, their affections will be totally estranged from it; and, sir, you know that a government, without their affections, can neither be durable nor happy. I speak as one poor individual; but when I speak, I speak the language of thousands. But, sir, I mean not to breathe the spirit, nor utter the language, of secession.

I have trespassed so long on your patience, I am really concerned that I have something yet to say. The honorable member has said, we shall be properly represented. Remember, sir, that the number of our representatives is but ten, whereof six is a majority. Will those men be possessed of sufficient information? A particular knowledge of particular districts will not suffice. They must be well acquainted with agriculture, commerce, and a great variety of other matters throughout the continent; they must know not only the actual state of nations in Europe and America, the situations of their farmers, cottagers, and mechanics, but also the relative situations and intercourse of those nations. Virginia is as large as England. Our proportion of representatives is but ten men. In England they have five hundred and fifty-eight. The House of Commons, in England, numerous as they are, we are told, are bribed, and have bartered away the rights of their constituents: what, then, shall become of us? Will these few protect our rights? Will they be incorruptible? You say they will be better men than the English commoners. I say they will be infinitely worse men, because they are to be chosen blindfolded: their election (the term, as applied to their appointment, is inaccurate) will be an involuntary nomination, and not a choice.

I have, I fear, fatigued the committee; yet I have not said the one hundred thousandth part of what I have on my mind, and wish to impart. On this occasion, I conceived myself bound to attend strictly to the interest of the state, and I thought her dearest rights at stake. Having lived so long—been so much honored—my efforts, though small, are due to my country. I have found my mind hurried on, from subject to subject, on this very great occasion. We have been all out of order, from the gentleman who opened to-day to myself. I did not come prepared to speak, on so multifarious a subject, in so general a manner. I trust you will indulge me another time. Before you abandon the present system, I hope you will consider not only its defects, most maturely, but likewise those of that which you are to substitute for it. May you be fully apprized of the dangers of the latter, not by fatal experience, but by some abler advocate than I!

PHOTO AND ILLUSTRATION CREDITS

★ ★ ★